NO MORE THAN FIVE IN A BED

COLORADO HOTELS IN THE OLD DAYS

No More Than FIVE In A Bed

COLORADO HOTELS IN THE OLD DAYS

BY SANDRA DALLAS

UNIVERSITY OF OKLAHOMA PRESS : NORMAN

BY SANDRA DALLAS

Gaslights and Gingerbread (Denver, 1965)
No More Than Five in a Bed: Colorado Hotels in the Old Days
(Norman, 1967)

LIBRARY OF CONGRESS CATALOG CARD NUMBER: 67–15587

TO HARRIETT MAVITY DALLAS

WHO SHOWED ME THE VIEW
FROM A DIAMOND-DUST MIRROR

RULES OF THIS HOUSE

1. Don't shoot the pianist; he's doing his damndest.

2. Please don't swear, damn you.

3. Beds, 50¢; with sheets, 75¢.

4. No horses above the first floor.

5. No more than five in a bed.

6. Warmth provided by horse blankets, liquor, and Christian zeal.

7. Funerals on the house.

ACKNOWLEDGMENTS

No writer could possibly complete historical work about Colorado without acknowledging a great debt to Mrs. Enid T. Thompson, head librarian of the Colorado State Historical Society, and her kind staff, Mrs. Laura A. Ekstrom for a mammoth job of researching, Mrs. Louisa Ward Arps, whose history comes out in entertaining conversations, and Mrs. Kay Pierson, who kept hotels in the back of her photographic mind for us for many months; and to Mrs. Alys Freeze, head librarian of the Western History Department, Denver Public Library, and her equally diligent staff—Mrs. Opal Harber, Mrs. Mary Hanley, Mrs. Hazel Lundberg, and Miss Eileen White—and to James Davis for spotting photographs in unlikely places. I am also indebted to Richard W. Purdie, University of Denver photographer, for making good prints from many a stained old photograph; to historians Fred and Jo Mazzula for pictures and fascinating bits of information dropped in conversation; and to Duane Howell, *Denver Post* photographer, for dredging up old photographs of the Windsor taken for a college class, that started all this.

I owe a great deal of gratitude to those legend tenders Harriet M. Alexander, Salida's *grande dame;* Rene Coquoz, a favorite Leadville pal; Helen Rich and Belle Turnbull, two mentors with a cache of Breckenridge bits and pieces; and Vivian Richardson, Cripple Creek's story keeper.

Special thanks must go to those who helped with field work: Mrs. Laurence M. Elisha in Aspen; E. N. Howard, Boulder; Guenther Hofeditz, charming proprietor of the Ore Bucket, Edna Enyeart, Marion Griffin, and Mrs. Jane Porter Robertson in

Breckenridge; Fred Sindt, that worthy of the Broadmoor; E. L. Bennett and Lillian Hargroves Campbell in Creede; Otto Lentz, H. O. Wood, and Francis S. Young, Canon City; Margaret Ackelbein, Guy White, Dorr Woolwine, and Dorothy and Wayne S. Mackin, who have set off a second gold rush to Cripple Creek; remarkable Dana Crawford and her fine assistants, Dee Manning and Ruth Sumners, as well as John Fishback, and Bertha Berger, Larimer Square, Denver; Myrtle Andrean, Earl A. Barker, Jr., Josie M. Crum, George Vest Day, and A. E. Lundy in Durango; R. W. Dean, Estes Park; Louise C. Harrison, Empire; Mrs. Ona Anderson of the Hotel de Paris and Mrs. Paul Atchison, Colonial Dame and constant helper, Georgetown; *Rocky Mountain News* writer Pat Hanna, as great a fan of Barbara and Frank Finn at Gold Hill as I am; Hazel E. Johnson, Greeley; C. J. Lessard, Leadville; R. L. Coghill and Mabel Willie in Manitou Springs; Marjorie Lankford for an entertaining morning at Poncha Springs; Mrs. Joan Beattie, Ouray; Virgil Mason and, of course, William A. Way in Silverton; Rossie F. Homer and again Clay Monson and Ann Rich in Steamboat Springs; Fannie Ball, Alta M. Cassietto, Mrs. Harry J. Johnson, Donald O'Rourke, Frank B. Thomas, and Russell Winn, Telluride; Mr. and Mrs. Floyd Beauchamp and Mr. and Mrs. Edward Howard, past and present proprietors of the Columbian in Trinidad; William Millikin, David Downs, and Lillian Titmas, Victor's history vanguards.

SANDRA DALLAS

Denver, Colorado
March 13, 1967

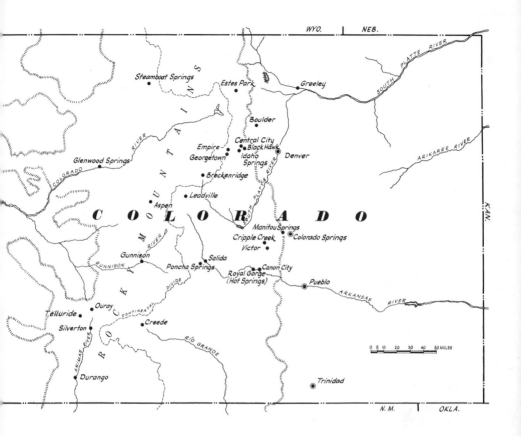

TABLE OF CONTENTS

Part III—Spas and Watering Spots

MAP

EARLY HOTELS

1. "More of Casey's Tabble Dote"
(Gold Hill Inn)

When dapper Eugene Field was a Denver newspaperman, he penned a collection of poems about a town he called "Red Hoss Mountain" and the "high-toned restauraw" he dubbed "Casey's":

> *And Casey's tabble dote began in French,—as all begin,—*
> *And Casey's ended with the same, which is to say, with "vin";*
> *But in between wuz every kind of reptile, bird, 'nd beast,*
> *The same like you can git in high-toned restauraws down East;*
> *'Nd windin' up wuz cake or pie, with coffee demy tass,*
> *Or, sometimes, floatin' Ireland in a soothin kind of sass*
> *That left a sort of pleasant ticklin' in a feller's throat,*
> *'Nd made him hanker after more of Casey's tabble dote.*

Well, there really was a Casey's—there still is. Back then it was the Miners' Hotel, better known as the Wentworth House; now it's the Gold Hill Inn, a barn-sized chinked-log structure on top of Horsfall Mountain in a town named Gold Hill.

Just outside Boulder, Gold Hill was one of the first of Colorado's mining camps. The precious metal was discovered there in 1859, and within a few years' time, over three thousand gold seekers had settled in the prosperous town, rough but not wide-open. Despite its name of "Miners' Hotel," the Wentworth House was built not as a boardinghouse for local men but as a tourist hotel with an outstanding "tabble dote." Colorado's hotel man Charles Wentworth, "late of Central and Denver," the poem's Casey, built the Wentworth House in 1873 "in first-class style." Though constructed of clapboard-covered hand-hewn logs in a "substantial style," the Wentworth House was a formal hotel with parlor and reading room, a small dining room, an elaborate bridal suite, and thirty bedrooms. It was the "only hotel in the city having anything but *hay* beds."

Eugene Field discovered the hotel early, and in 1874, under the pseudonym "Pick," described it in the *Denver Tribune*:

61251

The Wentworth House, with its huge, cheerful and old-fashioned "fireplaces" reminds one of the good "old days" when wood was worth but its cutting, and one may travel Colorado over before he finds better accommodations than mine host Wentworth provides for all his guests.

A frequent guest at the hotel, Eugene Field always slept in the same room—the only bedroom in the hotel connecting with the one next to it.

When the gold played out, so did Gold Hill and the Wentworth House, too. The hotel was closed for many years, but since Gold Hill was on the way to nowhere, and few people passed through the town, nobody bothered the old building. Then sometime in the early 1920's, Emma Tracy, head of an organization for Chicago working girls called the "Bluebirds," purchased the Wentworth House, added a building for a dining hall, and turned the complex into a summer camp for single women. The Bluebirds charged $6.50 a week in 1920 plus $25.00 for a round-trip railroad ticket from Chicago. In 1925 the cost of board and room had been raised to $12.00 a week, and by 1960 it had jumped to $35.00.

Shortly after the camp opened, Miss Tracy invited orator Clarence Darrow to speak to the girls. The famous lawyer accepted the invitation enthusiastically and took the train to Boulder to meet Miss Tracy. Driving to the camp, the pair passed an abandoned cabin with a good screen door, and since the hotel needed just such a piece Miss Tracy looked at it longingly and remarked, "How I'd like to have that door!"

Darrow replied, "You go over and get it. I'll act as your defense attorney."

"No," said Miss Tracy. "I'm not strong enough to handle it. You bring it over." So Darrow climbed out of the car, ripped off the door, and took it to the camp with them.

Darrow visited the camp several times, and the highlight of each visit came as the girls sat around Wentworth's old dining room table and listened as the orator recited "Casey's Tabble Dote."

Nearly four thousand women stayed at the Bluebirds' camp in Gold Hill during the forty years it was operated. Towards the end, however, only a few showed up each summer. The appeal of traveling in groups had ended; women had begun to vacation by themselves, and the idea of a summer camp had lost its excitement. In the early 1960's the Bluebirds sold the camp to an Eastern couple. The pair, enthralled by Field's poem, opened a restaurant in the dining hall and patterned its menu around "Casey's Tabble Dote." They decorated the restaurant, renamed the "Gold Hill Inn," in early gold-camp *décor*, not the fashionable flashy Victorian plush but the old Gold Hill style—a sort of studied tackiness.

The atmosphere has a look now of mining camp *objets d'art*: battered antique chairs still graceful, their backs carved in delicate ovals; a wizened mine bellows; a gauzy green Tiffany lamp shade. An old organ stands regally in the foyer, its keys turned the yellow of autumn aspen leaves, its tone the cry of the wind in winter. A once-devastating plaster Venus with a sordid past looks down from the mantel. The armless lady once was the prized possession of a Sunshine Canyon miner named Snowbound Charlie. He kept her chained to a tree in front of his house and decorated her at Christmastime with a string of beer cans. The unaesthetic Bluebirds spirited her away one night and hid her in their basement where she moldered until later owners discovered her and gave her a place above their fireplace.

The dining room, still heated by the highly polished giant of a cookstove, is filled with mix-matched tables covered with ripply seersucker cloths, stiff bandana napkins, bits of mountain flowers —wild asters, strawberry blossoms, slippery kinnikinnick—and candle stubs stuck into ancient tin mugs.

Several years after they opened the restaurant, the owners decided to reopen the old hotel. They refurbished the building, added antique furniture, new fireplaces, and coal stoves, and even a hip tub in the bathroom.

5

The Wentworth House (*top*), the original "Casey's" (*Denver Public Library Western Collection*). Today's Casey's, the Gold Hill Inn.

The rooms are attractive with a lazy kind of mountain charm, but, as in Field's day, it is the "restauraw" with roast suckling pig, roast goose, and coffee "demy tass" that leaves " a sort of pleasant ticklin' in a feller's throat" and makes him "hanker after more."

6

2. The Principal Hotel at the Present Time *(Jackson)*

Travelers visiting remote areas of early Colorado were so accustomed to sleeping on the ground or in the coarse beds of occasional way stations that they looked forward with relief to the clean and comfortable Jackson Hotel in Poncha Springs. A few of the Jackson's guests, such as John D. Rockefeller, were used to luxurious trappings at home, though they were glad enough to settle for the Jackson's homespun sheets and handmade quilts. For the most part, however, the men who registered at the Jackson Hotel were railroad workers and miners and occasionally outlaws who found the hotel's rooms far more comfortable than their customary night's surroundings on the prairie or the side of a mountain.

Henry A. Jackson built his hotel in Poncha in 1878, when there was talk of turning the curative warm-water springs into a resort attraction. Evidently not one to speculate, Jackson did not build a resort hotel for an elusive tourist crowd but rather a simple, substantial hotel stop for everyday travelers. The Jackson was a two-story building with a lobby and dining room on the first floor, a few bedrooms on the second. Later a wing was added, bringing the number of sleeping rooms to thirty-one. The lobby's one luxury was an elaborately carved rosewood grand piano which had been hauled across the plains by oxcart. The bedrooms contained a few walnut and sample bedsteads though for the most part they were iron, and the only other adornments were the usual bowl, pitcher, and chamber pot.

Discovered by Kit Carson, the springs at Poncha Pass, which numbered close to sixty, could accommodate forty thousand visitors daily, according to an enthusiastic brochure printed in the early 1880's. It claimed, "A great variety of diseases are cured by the peculiar *earth heated and medicated waters* and intelligent system of baths. The effect on the sick is wonderfully beneficial, corrollating a special energy with the climate and pure atmosphere."

The problem with Poncha was its lack of an elegant hotel. The rooms at the Jackson were good enough for passers-by, but they weren't quite fancy enough for the health seekers from Leadville and Buena Vista. The springs attracted fifteen to twenty visitors a day, according to an 1879 newspaper account, "but as there were no accommodations, they passed on." *Crofutt's Gripsack Guide* reported, "A small hotel and a half a dozen tents are provided for boarders or families who wish to . . . enjoy the waters." A more disdainful account declared, "The Jackson House is the principal hotel at the present time . . . a first-class hotel will be built at an early date."

Despite predictions, the Jackson remained the best hotel in Poncha Springs. No one put up the capital to build the first-class hotel, and as a result, tourists who wanted to spend the night at the springs had to stay in the homy rooms of the Jackson. Though a few health seekers persisted in visiting Poncha Springs and staying at the Jackson, the hotel found that its real bread-and-butter customers were the crossroads traffic, the guests who went through Poncha Springs, not to it.

The Jackson sent its sprightly painted wagon to the narrow-gauge station to meet suffrage leader Susan B. Anthony, who spent the night in the hotel and gave a lecture in its dining room. Guests as different as Rudyard Kipling, Ulysses S. Grant, and Alexander Graham Bell signed the register as did local celebrities such as Evelyn Walsh McLean and Lieutenant Governor H. A. W. Tabor, who later built a shack near the springs for private use. Outlaws Frank and Jesse James, allegedly hiding out from Missouri and Colorado law officers, were said to have found Jackson, who was supposed to have been a neighbor in Missouri, a welcoming host. Local legend also claims that Jackson gave Frank James a sound thrashing for abusing the proprietor's horse—and got away with it. Another doubtful guest to sign the Jackson register was William Bonney, better known as Billy the Kid, who would have needed three lives to be in all the places he was supposed to be, this one included.

As the leading hotel in Poncha Springs, the Jackson also was the favorite place to eat. A grocery bill still kept by the hotel, issued in 1886 by Appleby and Abright General Merchandise, lists six pounds of beef, three and one-half pounds of bacon, and ten pounds of onions for a total charge of $1.87. Fifty pounds of flour cost $1.45 and candles used to light the hotel were $.20 a dozen. A bill from Sprague and Smith Meat Market charged $4.00 for thirty-two pounds of beef, $2.88 for twenty-three pounds of pork.

For many years the Jackson remained just an overnight stop. It never operated as a resort, and it wasn't elegant enough to attract fashionable guests other than those who had business in Poncha. In later years when automobile travel became common, the Jackson catered to tourists and fishermen who wanted to spend a few days in the area.

Today the once-fenced front yard contains gas pumps; the dining room is a café. An additional room was built on the front to house the hotel's collection of relics, and the proprietor proudly points out the bed where the James brothers are supposed to have slept, the false-bottom chair in which they kept their guns and liquor, and the register book open to their signatures, rubbed faint by the hundreds of tourists who have touched them.

On the mountain across from the Jackson the hot springs were enclosed in a round, wood shanty. A second hotel, a facsimile of the Jackson called the Poncha House, stood near by. (*Collection of Fred and Jo Mazzulla*)

The current Jackson lives mostly on past glory.

3. Things of Which the Old Peck House Has Boasted *(Splendide)*

Prospectors and pioneers headed for the promising land on the western side of the Berthoud Pass would pause for a moment as they started up the steep slope for a last glimpse of civilization, the town of Empire. A fortunate few might rest from their travels at the home of the James Pecks before attacking the mountains, and enjoy what might be their last meal at a table or night in a bed.

Known all over the area for their hospitality, the Pecks were kind, friendly people. Their home, certainly the finest in Empire, welcomed not only the straggling pioneers on their way farther west but many of the Eastern magnates who ventured to the town to investigate the Empire mines for possible investment.

The home was owned by James Peck, a successful Chicago merchant who had arrived in Empire in the early 1860's with his sons, to prospect for gold. In a short time he had found one of Empire's most productive veins, located on Silver Mountain. The house he had built for himself and his sons when they first arrived in Empire, a four-room frame building, was later given a stone foundation and enlarged to two stories. Peck added a banister hand-hewn from a single pine tree and a primitive pipeline made of thousands of one-inch pieces of aspen hollowed out with a hot poker, to carry water from the spring to the house, a quarter-mile away.

When all was finished, Peck sent for his fashionable wife and daughters, who brought with them to the gold camp walnut and oak furniture, much of it Louis XIV style, china, silver, linen, a collection of books, and a fifteen-pound Bible. In addition, Mrs. Peck set up housekeeping in Empire with a collection of exquisite jewelry and sixteen full-skirted dresses.

Another unusual piece which Mrs. Peck decided to have ox-freighted across the prairie to the high mountain town was a brass ship bell from a Lake Michigan vessel. The bell, which was hung above the Pecks' front door, rang breakfast, high noon, and dinner and later announced the arrival of the tri-weekly hack from Central City.

Since the Peck home was the nicest in Empire, it was only natural that the Peck family would put up travelers, but only if they were well known to the family or highly recommended by friends. Many guests were Eastern investors anxious to explore the Colorado mines; others were pioneers who had traveled hundreds of miles across the prairies to sleep for the first time in weeks in real beds, provided by the Pecks.

Emma Shepard Hill, an early Empire resident, recalled journeying many months across the plains with her family to reach Empire. With her parents she entered the Peck home, "a large living room with open fireplace, piled high with blazing logs, dimming the light of several kerosene lamps, and a glimpse into the room beyond where a bounteous meal was spread on a table, a real table."

For nearly ten years, until the early 1870's, the Pecks invited travelers into their home, giving them board and bed without charge. But by the seventies, Empire was in a depression; the Pecks, like everybody else, felt a financial slack. By then, too, most of the Peck children had married and moved away, so the outgoing Mrs. Peck was lonely in the big house. The Pecks decided then to add a modest charge to the hospitality which they had given so freely for a decade and turned their home into a hotel, the Peck House.

Many years before, while in Chicago, the Pecks had lived in hotels, and during their ten years of hosting travelers, the couple had learned a good deal about boarding guests, so they entered the inn business not as novices but practically as professionals.

Inspired by a particular Chicago hotel in which she had lived, Mrs. Peck decided to hire a French chef to take care of the dining room. But the impracticality of the idea (there was no cook, let alone a French one, who could be hired) soon made it clear that Mrs. Peck and a daughter-in-law living with the family would do most of the kitchen work. As far as guests were concerned, no Frenchman was needed. Mrs. Peck was a fine pastry cook—her specialty was wild berry torte—and the two women turned out an impressive menu. Roast beef dinner sold for forty cents, a T-bone was fifty, and lobster, when it was offered, cost a full dollar. Even oysters were available, and one Christmas the Pecks hung their Christmas trees with fried oysters.

In 1880, James Peck, not only a hotel man but mayor, postmaster, and station agent as well as "emperor" of Empire, died. His son Frank gave up a job as Georgetown station agent to help his mother operate the Peck House. Young Frank Peck began making changes almost immediately. A mid-December edition of the *Daily News,* an Empire newspaper, noted:

> Prop. Frank L. Peck, of the famous Peck house, has completed the addition to his house at the cost of $2000. It is 35 x 40 feet and two stories in height. The upstairs is divided into bedrooms and the lower into a reading room, office, and billiard parlor. A handsome billiard table has just been put up. The Daily News can always be found there.

The addition, built by the man who had constructed the original portion of the hotel, along with a few changes made in 1887, turned the Peck House into an attractive building. The hotel was white clapboard with a two-story veranda running the length of the house and around the side. The interior was fashionably decorated. Wainscoting in many of the rooms was made of wide pine boards alternately colored with dark and light stain. Thick leather chairs stood in the lobby. French windows were spaced across the front of the house to let in the vast southern view.

The Peck House was the first building in town to have electricity, powered by a water wheel. Later the Pecks bought a motor to generate not only their own electricity but the town's as well. Empire residents always knew when the generator was turned on because the red, white, and blue lights strung across the front of the hotel began to flicker. Promptly at midnight, the Pecks turned off the generator, and electricity was off until the following evening. A phone line was installed in the Peck House in 1881, and to celebrate the event Empire and Georgetown held a joint telephone concert.

Soon after Frank Peck took over the hotel it became a popular spot for the "gay Georgetown crowd," which attended card parties, hops, even wedding receptions in the hotel's public rooms. Women liked to flirt or gossip in the ladies' lounge while the young men played billiards or drank at the bar, staffed by a man named Mix.

Not only local people but visiting dignitaries signed the black oilcloth register book in the lobby. P. T. Barnum stayed in the Peck House while he was in Empire. Colorado's epicurean Senator Edward Wolcott was a guest. Generals John A. Logan and traveling companion William Tecumseh Sherman signed the guest book beside the puzzling signature of President Ulysses S. Grant. As far as anyone can tell, Grant never stopped at the Peck House; in fact, he never visited Empire. The signature is not in his handwriting, but his name is there, right beside the names of his two generals.

Until the turn of the century, the Peck House was a fashionable, pleasant place to stay. "Neatness, comfort and good living, together with the prettiest mountain outlook to be found in Colorado, are things of which the Old Peck House has boasted," declared an Idaho Springs newspaper.

But though it could boast of itself as a comfortable place to stay, the Peck House couldn't fight loss of business when Empire's gold mining declined. The once-grand hotel became a shabby stop for fishermen and occasional tourists. It operated as a second-class establishment for many years, and most of its fine furnishings were sold to pay taxes.

In the 1940's, after the Peck House had been in the Peck family nearly ninety years, Mr. Joe Emerson Smith purchased the place and attempted to restore it. In the 1950's he sold it to two women, Louise C. Harrison and her sister, Margaret Colibran, who began the hotel's major renovation. They replaced plumbing and electricity, added bathrooms and closets. The two had furniture refinished and reupholstered, walls torn down and rooms rearranged. When they were finished, the Peck House, renamed the "Hotel Splendide," stood a grand imitation of its former fashionable self.

Today guests step into the hotel on a claret-colored carpet and enter a lobby furnished with handsome antiques. One room has been turned into an ice-cream parlor with delicate iron chairs and candy-striped wallpaper. The dining room, the only addition to the Peck House in seventy years, still has one of the original hotel's rope leg tables. Frosted-glass light globes bearing the Colorado state seal, which once lit the halls of the state capitol, now illumine the Splendide dining room. Bedrooms have been carpeted and re-papered with Victorian designs and display walnut chests and iron bedsteads.

The Peck House, which in its multicolored history has gone from family home to fashionable hotel to neglected lodginghouse and back again to excellent hostelry, boasts of being the oldest continually operated hotel in Colorado, and chances are it will be for a long time.

GREETINGS from Hotel SPLENDIDE 1964

the original PECK HOUSE, 1864 EMPIRE, COLORADO

The original Peck House (*above*) before it was turned into a hotel. Mr. and Mrs. Frank Peck and their son Frank (*center*) are somewhere among the crowd on the front porch (*Library, State Historical Society of Colorado*). Renamed the Hotel Splendide (*bottom*), the hotel looked little different from the original Peck House. A portion of the section to the left is the only addition to the hotel in seventy years.

4. May the Soul of John Zang Rest in Peace
   (Creede)

The scraggly, stuccoed-over hotel, two nameless shades of brown, cowering like the rest of Creede beneath massive river-cut cliffs, has a prosaic look, an austere, workaday air, but beneath its unadorned surface lie an inner pensiveness and a hundred stories that made Creede one of Colorado's most fabulous gold camps.

The hotel was built around 1888, but not until 1892, when John Zang took it over, is there a mention in history of who might have owned it. The immigrant Zang and his wife left their German homeland several years before, in the early 1880's, to venture to Georgetown, Colorado, where they opened a mine camp boardinghouse. A year of that and the couple moved to Denver to build a splendid three-story brick hotel at Thirty-sixth and Market streets, patronized by Union Pacific railroaders. In 1892, Zang and his wife went to Creede and took over operation of one of the hotels there. Like the one in Denver, the Creede hotel was named the "Zang" after its proprietor. The couple ran the hotel, predecessor of the current one, for a couple of years; then suddenly it was swept away in the first of Creede's big fires. Undaunted by the ill fortune, the plucky German built a second Zang Hotel on the site of the first.

Slightly smaller than its predecessor, the second Zang was a rectangular two-story building with a fancy pillastered veranda. It had a lobby, dining room, and saloon, all combined, with a kitchen behind. Upstairs were the unadorned bedrooms. Next to the hotel was a one-story building which advertised on its half-curtained windows that it was the Zang Hotel office, reading room, and barbershop with twenty-five-cent baths.

Though the Zang considered itself a respectable establishment and employed a man just to keep rowdies out of the bar, it ran a string of cribs behind the hotel, a brick row of tiny rooms opening off a long porch. When not in use by prostitutes, the rooms sometimes served as dressing quarters for dance-hall girls.

The higher class women of Creede shunned the back rooms and lived upstairs in the hotel—Poker Alice Tubbs and Killarney Kate, two cigar-smoking female cardsharks who worked in Creede's gambling dens. Another was the woman who followed Bob Ford from Missouri.

The "dirty little coward [who] shot Mr. Howard" was Bob Ford, who fled to Colorado after killing his cousin Jesse James. Though he traveled light, Ford managed to take along one piece of baggage—a female friend, whose name since has been lost. The couple rented a room upstairs at the Zang, and Bob went to work setting up his own tent saloon. Nobody much cared that Bob Ford had killed cousin Jesse except a man named Ed Kelly, out to build himself a reputation and anxious to latch onto Ford's woman at the same time. His notions got to be too much for Kelly, and one day he sauntered into Ford's saloon and shot the dirty little coward.

Creede folk hadn't paid much attention to Bob Ford while he was alive, but they got mighty concerned about him after he was shot and declared he was part of Creede's villainous element and couldn't be buried with the decent dead; he would have to be laid away in the plot set aside for the prostitutes. Ford's lady friend was so indignant at the insult to her dead lover that she had the newly buried body dug up and shipped over Slumgullion Pass to Lake City, then changed her mind and eventually sent the body to Missouri for final burial.

While all this was going on in Creede, John Zang and his wife quietly ran the Zang Hotel, renting rooms to the West's famous and infamous—Bat Masterson, a Creede peace officer for a time, and Soapy Smith, the gold rush's most affable con man. The Zangs had a good hotel; they operated it themselves for years and leased it occasionally. The couple saw the hotel through Creede's rough years to the gentler ones and planned to live out their lives quietly with the town until their plans died abruptly with John Zang one spring afternoon in 1911.

"MURDER! John Zang Shot and Instantly Killed by Mrs. Lefevre at her Residence," screamed the headlines of the *Creede Candle* on June 17, 1911:

> One of the most horrifying murders in the history of the Creede district occured last Sunday afternoon in the Stringtown portion of North Creede.
>
> John Zang, the well-known proprietor of the Zang hotel . . . was shot and almost instantly killed by Mrs. Michael Lefevre, who used a .45 calibre Colt's revolver, in her house on the North Creede road during the absence of her husband.
>
> It was a most horrible sight that met the gaze of the officers of the law. At the same time, as an example of supreme nerve it excelled anything this editor has ever seen.
>
> There upon the floor in the doorway between the bedroom and the kitchen lay the corpse of Mr. Zang with a bullet hole in his left cheek, almost on the cheek-bone, and the entire side of his face terribly burned with powder marks, showing that the gun must have been fired at a fearfully close range in order for the powder to have left such terrible marks. Beneath his head and surrounding it was a large pool of blood which had coagulated and had matted in his hair. Standing at the side table in the kitchen was Mrs. Lefevre, calmly and unconcernedly washing the dishes as if nothing had ever happened out of the ordinary. Whenever she had occasion to go near the body there was never a shudder or a tremble, never a token of fear or repugnance nor the flicker of an eyelid to denote that she knew or felt of its presence.

In a statement made to the *Candle* editor, Mrs. Lefevre claimed that Zang had come to her house when she was alone and had tried to "mistreat me." When she refused him and ordered him from the house, Zang "dragged me into the bedroom and threw me on the bed. I jumped up and ran out into the kitchen grabbing the gun as I ran. I pointed it at him and told him four times to go. He struck me in the face and bruised my eye. I ordered him out four times and when he again tried to seize me, I shot him and killed him."

The editor noted somewhat skeptically that "Mr. Zang's side of the story will never be known," and predicted that "the evidence given by the self-confessed murderess was of sufficient strength to cause a jury to claim that the shot was fired in self-defense and thus acquit the woman of premeditation—which the jury apparently did. "May the soul of John Zang rest in peace, is the wish of all who knew him,"concluded the *Candle*.

Though Mrs. Zang's "spirit seems to be utterly broken by the fearful calamity," and "her grief became uncontrollable and she obtained possession of a revolver . . . and attempted to make away with herself," she soon rallied and continued to run the hotel after her husband's death. Then a few years later, in a brief article dated September 20, 1919, the *Candle* noted that Mrs. Zang had sold her hotel, and two months later gave the reason in a wedding announcement. Her grief was consolable, after all. She married William Orthen and moved away.

After a variety of owners (the ghost of one occasionally walks across the snow-covered hotel roof without leaving footprints) the Zang, renamed the "Creede Hotel," was sold to Lillian Hargraves Campbell. Hotel restoration came naturally to her—a sister remodeled both the Windsor in Denver and the Strathmore in Canon City—and she has restored the never-lavish hotel to its nevertheless comfortable former self, where one may, indeed, rest in peace.

John Zang's hotel when Creede was booming (*Library, State Historical Society of Colorado*).

The Creede Hotel today claims more infamy than the Zangs liked to boast.

5. By the Week Cheaper *(Gilpin)*

When President Ulysses S. Grant, visiting in Gregory Gulch during one of his periodic whirlwind trips through Colorado's mining towns, stepped off the narrow gauge at Black Hawk, he headed for the best hotel. Informed by the excited head of a welcoming delegation that the town had planned a grand entertainment in his honor, the weary President replied, "Entertainment, hell! I haven't slept for two days; I'm going to bed." And he made his way to the Gilpin Hotel where he did just that.

The tale is a good one, and it is somewhat typical of Grant; what a pity that it probably isn't true. There is no record that the President ever visited Black Hawk, and if he did, he probably

20

headed up the hill to spend the night at Central City's Teller House. But the tale persists, and like most of the legends of the camps, it's a good story for what it is worth.

Another tale told about the Gilpin, equally dubious, is that Horace Greeley, touring Colorado in 1860, visited the Gregory diggings and checked into the Gilpin. While staying there, so the story goes, he was prompted to write his famous "Go West" article for the *New York Tribune*.

There are a number of readily available facts about the Gilpin, sworn to be true, but, alas, they are not nearly so interesting as the legends. The back portion of the present-day hotel, made of hewn logs, was built in 1859 or 1860 and operated as Black Hawk's first school, until 1869 when the town built another. At one time the building may have housed a newspaper, but nobody knows when or even what one.

Along about 1896 the hotel's owner at the time, Julius Kline, moved the old clapboard-covered log building back off the street and built a new hotel in front of it. The three-story sand brick structure had forty plain rooms, each with a tiny stove. "At the present time the house has forty regular boarders. Transient trade is always welcomed here and special rooms are set aside for them," reported a local souvenir booklet published around 1900, though it didn't add where the special rooms might be since, as it noted, the forty were permanently filled.

The booklet continued that of the many hotels in Black Hawk, the Gilpin "easily takes front rank." The hotel was described as attractive, "and the office is large and inviting. The guest chambers are neat, clean and airy, the beds are first class, and the table set, for excellence, cannot be surpassed." Rooms rented for $1.00 to $1.25 per day, "and by the week cheaper."

The Gilpin never was a hotel for long-term owners, and it was constantly up for sale. The list of managers included a new name every few years. For the most part those names are unfamiliar, though the hotel at one time was run by the O'Toole family, later managers of famous Denver and Colorado Springs hotels.

In later years when Black Hawk began feeling the surge of tourist popularity of its neighbor-up-the-hill Central, the Gilpin was refurbished in popular pseudo-Victorian style—pretty pink walls stenciled with crimson designs and gilded with paper gold seals. The hotel was decorated—probably more elaborately than it had been in its earlier days—with gaslight chandeliers and plush furniture. The basement storage area was turned into a rathskeller called the "Mine Shaft Bar." The Gilpin's current success, much as in past days, is sporadic though optimistic, and once again the hotel is up for sale.

The Gilpin Hotel in the 1890's, shortly after the brick portion of the building was built. (*Denver Public Library Western Collection*).

The Gilpin as it appears now.

PART II

VICTORIAN HOTELS

6. Best Place to Dine on the D&RG
(Monte Cristo)

When the Denver & Rio Grande threaded its way into Salida, the future supply point of the Colorado mining camps, the town had no decent hotel, and it appeared as though nobody had plans for one, so the railroad built its own. And the hotel, the Monte Cristo, was known up and down the line as the best place to dine on the D&RG.

Far from a pretentious Victorian hotel, the Monte Cristo looked like a typical railroad building whose depot-like lines were broken only by a tower and a few herringbone diagonal strips of dark-colored wood. Painted a bilious railroad yellow, the hotel was frame, three stories in one spot, two in another.

Though the Monte Cristo, which stood only a few feet from the railroad tracks, was strictly a D&RG product outside, inside it had the feel of a pleasant, late nineteenth-century hotel. The first story and the stairways were finished in ash, the second floor in pine. The $8,000 worth of furnishings, which brought the total cost of the hotel to $30,000, were of cherry, ash, and black walnut. Brussels carpets were used on the floor.

The first floor contained the office, reading room, sample room, dining room, lunchroom, kitchen, and porters' rooms. Above were twenty-five bedrooms fitted with steam heat, patent locks on the doors, and transoms. The Monte Cristo rooms weren't much, though an advertisement in the *Year Book of Churches of the Ascension in Salida, Colorado,* declared that the Monte Cristo was the "only first class hotel in the city." What really made the Monte Cristo special was its dining room. Supplied by kitchens both on the first floor and in the basement, the hotel dining room, decorated with gaslights and shutters, could seat close to one hundred and offered an elaborate menu.

The Monte Cristo had no ceremonial opening. Passengers just alighted from the 11:25 A.M. Pacific Express one day in May,

1883, and trooped into the dining room for what passed as the hotel's grand opening.

Although the Monte Cristo served an impressive array of food every day, nothing ever surpassed the Christmas, 1886, menu. The hotel featured as entrees Blue Point oysters, California salmon with butter sauce, boiled ham with champagne sauce, boiled tongue, roast loin of beef, turkey with cranberry sauce, saddle of elk with currant jelly, canvasback duck, croquette of chicken in cream sauce, tenderloin of venison brazed, oyster patties, and fresh lobster.

Side dishes were oxtail soup, celery and radishes, pineapple fritters, French peas, sweet corn, mashed potatoes, sweet potatoes, and Hubbard squash. And for dessert there were steamed plum pudding with brandy sauce, lemon meringue, mince and pumpkin pies; macaroons, charlotte russe, vanilla ice cream, Turkey Elna, figs, Malaga grapes, oranges, assorted nuts, raisins, Edam cheese, and biscuits, besides Roman punch, St. Julian claret, and cider.

There is a legend current that Rudyard Kipling spent some time at the Monte Cristo, but ascertainable facts do not bear it out. Kipling did cross Colorado in 1889, but there is no written record of a stop at the hotel. It is true, however, that Miss Caroline Wolcott Ballestier, whom he married in 1892, was a guest there in 1883–84, visiting a friend, Miss Amy Graves, whose mother ran the Monte Cristo.

The D&RG never attempted to run the Monte Cristo itself but leased it to a series of managers, among them Judge C. F. Catlin, who lived at the hotel with his Newfoundland dog Duke. Each afternoon the dog would meet the westbound mail train and pick up a newspaper to deliver to an old lady on the opposite side of town. One day as the train approached the depot Duke saw something fall into its path, raced up the tracks, and pulled a two-year-old girl from in front of the train. The little child was saved, but Duke was struck by the train and killed, and many years later the Salida Junior Chamber of Commerce erected a monument on Tenderfoot Mountain, directly behind the Monte Cristo, dedicated to the memory of "a faithful dog."

The quality of the Monte Cristo dining room started slipping when the trains began providing passengers with good dining facilities on board, and the rooms began deteriorating when travelers preferred Pullman accommodations on the railroad to overnight stops. By the end of World War I, the dining room was closed, and all that was left was a lunch counter. Most of the rooms were turned into railroad offices not long after that. Shortly after World War II, the Monte Cristo, which had long outlived its usefulness, was torn down.

W. H. Jackson photographed most of the famous and infamous buildings in Colorado, including the Monte Cristo (*Denver Public Library Western Collection*).

7. A Barroom Conveniently Adjunct *(Victor)*

"Victor Hotel lobby—any night" is the inscription scrawled on back of an old photograph. The picture shows a reluctant group of motley miners and businessmen backed against the rear of the room to make space for the photographer. Behind them is a list of local merchants, a reminder to hotel guests that the City of Mines was a straightforward, businesslike city.

Like its town, Victor was a steady, sturdy, no-nonsense kind of place. It was sensibly built, devoid of the frivolities of its competitors in other cities. And the Victor was a money-maker, too. In fact, it brought its builders a fortune even before the foundation was poured.

The two Woods brothers, Frank and Harry, founding fathers of Victor, whose Woods Investment Company owned the lion's share of the town, began excavating for the hotel in the mid-1890's. While crews were digging the foundation, a wandering assayer, curious about the composition of the earth and rock which the workmen were dumping to the side, took a sample, inspected it, and told the Woods brothers that their hotel was about to cover one of the area's most promising veins. Sure enough, the Woods boys stopped construction on the hotel to drive a shaft and begin mining operations on the hotel site. They named their discovery the Gold Coin, and it produced so much money for the pair that their investment company nearly ran out of projects in which to invest. At its peak the bonanza which they had found on the slope of Battle Mountain brought them $30,000 a month.

Fortunately for the Victor Hotel, the vein discovered in its basement caused only a temporary delay in the building's construction. Crews soon began grading a foundation on the less minerally rich Victor Avenue at the corner of Fourth Street, a few hundred feet down the mountain from the original site, and erected the four-story hotel, the highest building in Victor.

The Victor Hotel was a rectangular building, devoid of embellishments, constructed of white pressed brick. The corner entrance, which led into the Bank of Victor, as well as the side-street entrance to the lobby, had small Romanesque arches, repeated three stories above in the fourth-floor windows. Brightly striped awnings shaded the first-floor windows.

Though admittedly plain, the Victor Hotel did have several embellishments. Its ceilings were intricately hammered metal. Elevator doors on the first floor were finely wrought black iron. A fluted-shell design was worked in the woodwork above entrances to some of the suites. The transoms were handsomely lettered with black and gold room numbers backed with gay paper designs.

The first floor, from the corner to the end of the Victor Avenue side, had been leased to the Bank of Victor. The floor above it was used as the local telephone exchange. Lawyers, doctors, engineers, and investors rented various rooms for business use.

At the same time, of course, the building carried on as Victor's finest hotel, rates $2.50 to $3.50 a day for a bed, a bath down the hall, and "courteous attendants with day and night clerks."

"Victor is blessed with a first-class hotel, and no one need be afraid to visit the 'City of Mines' and leave the comforts of home and good living, for here they are assured of the best in the land. In fact, the Hotel Victor furnishes as good service throughout as can be secured in Denver or any city west of Chicago," claimed an early-day magazine travel account.

Another said that the dining room service of the hotel was "unsurpassed anywhere in the state. A bar room is a convenient adjunct to the place."

The hotel made its biggest splash before it opened when the Gold Coin vein was discovered in the basement, and even after the building opened to admit travelers, it was more successful as something else. Most Victorites remember the Victor not as the town's best hotel but as a would-be mining exchange building and later as a hospital.

Never a hotel to compete with the posh and popular National in rivaling Cripple Creek on the other side of the mountain, the Victor entertained no celebrities, not even a well-known politician, let alone a vice-president. No mention can be found of a grand opening or fancy ball or any of the other fripperies that were the National's pride. The Victor Hotel was plain and sensible. It also was versatile, and while the National was torn down long ago because it couldn't pay for its foolishness, the Victor, admittedly deserted, at least still stands.

"Victor Hotel lobby—any night" (*Denver Public Library Western Collection*).

The derelict Victor, probably during the 1930's (*Glenn L. Gebhardt*).

8. Where the Wealth of the Earth Crops Out (*Oasis*)

The two-story pink building with the green shutters, shipped from Cheyenne in 1870, was considered Greeley's "aristocratic" hotel, far more respectable than the flea-ridden barn which some wag had named the "Hotel de Comfort." So it was quite a tragedy when the pretty pink place, called the "Greeley House," burned to the ground one sad day in 1880.

By the time of the fire there were other hotels in Greeley, of course. Prominent among them was the Barnum House, built on the orders of P. T. Barnum himself, who was an early investor in the young colony. But the Barnum House, with due respect to that popular and flamboyant showman, was generally considered somewhat more suited to transient circus troupes than to discriminating travelers. With the passing of the Greeley House, the town desperately needed a fine hotel.

So Greeley civic leaders took it as their duty to construct a hotel worthy of the fast-growing, respectable town, and they built the Oasis on the charred site of the Greeley House.

Three stories of brick, the Oasis faced a street corner and extended 108 feet east along one block, 36 feet south along another. It had a double-deck gallery on one side and a fancy design on the roof above the entrance with the name "Oasis" in raised letters. It was built and furnished for $85,000.

Inside were a lobby, a gentleman's parlor, two large sample rooms, a washroom, and a coatroom on the first floor along with the dining hall, kitchen, and town billiard hall. "The only billiard tables in Greeley are connected with the Oasis Hall," noted an early account, and they "have been run without bringing any trouble from liquor selling in connection."

Upstairs were the forty to fifty sleeping rooms, an elegant ladies' parlor, and a sparse number of bathrooms. "On each of the upper floors is a large water-closet, and above these the reservoir is connected with a standpipe, so water can be thrown into every part in case of fire," reported one newspaper. "We confidently claim that the Oasis surpasses any hotel outside of Denver, in point of comfort, convenience, decorations, and equipment."

Not long after the Oasis opened, David Boyd mentioned in his ponderous history of Greeley that many of the town's citizens had taken stock in the hotel "to start the enterprise, not expecting to get any pecuniary return. In this they were not disappointed, and were glad to give it up." Apparently when those early stockholders discovered that they were receiving no return on their investment, they were happy to sell, so the stock gradually filtered down to one man—who had no more success in running the Oasis than the horde that had preceded him.

During its early days, the Oasis apparently was only intermittently successful and once again, in 1896, the hotel changed hands. The "Oasis hotel served its last dinner this evening under the management of J. W. Purdy," reported the *Denver Republican*. "Its service and menu were excellent, but to no purpose. The patronage, both local and transient, was not sufficient to pay expenses, and the company ordered Mr. Purdy to close the house."

In 1906, D. A. Camfield purchased the Oasis, spent $35,000 remodeling, and much to the disgust of early-day residents chopped the "Oasis" off the top of the building and replaced it with "Camfield." The porch was removed and a veranda put in its place. Windows were changed, the lobby enlarged, and the floors tiled. Trees in front of the hotel were uprooted, to be replaced with giant clusters of ball lights. At one point another story was added. And the hotel began boasting on its stationery: "The place where the land is watered and the wealth of the earth crops out."

For all its changes, the Oasis, now the Camfield, charged its usual modest prices, fifty cents for lunch, sixty for dinner.

The hotel operated unpretentiously for many years, its dining room acting as a USO center during World War II. During the late 1950's an attempt was made to restore the Oasis. Then in 1964 the hotel of which all Greeley "may well be proud" was torn down.

The first hotel on the Oasis site was the Greeley, a Cheyenne hostelry shipped to Greeley in 1870 (*Denver Public Library Western Collection*).

Nobody recalls the event, but it must have been an important one since the Oasis was decked out in strips of bunting (*Hazel E. Johnson*).

9. Little Children Gazed In Wonder
(McClure)

Pioneer and poet laureate Governor Rudd (Anson S. Rudd never really *was* a Colorado governor, but he was nominated once for lieutenant governor) was so impressed with the McClure House in Canon City, every candle-lit window and leather-covered over-stuffed piece of it, that he was "inspired" to compose an eighteen-stanza poem in its honor and read it at the McClure's opening-night banquet:

> *What! Old Rudd here again with rhymes?*
> *I thought we'd fall'n on better times;*
> *That his old muse had fossilized,*
> *And time his wits had subsidized;*

But I suppose we'll hear him prate
 Of Canon City's future fate
Until old Charon doth deliver
 His soul across the mystic river.

You bet your life! I'm here again;
 I came in on a special train
By the Pueblo and Salt Lake route
 The latest thing, you know, that's out;
Which long's been agitated though,
 In our suburbs and Pueblo.
And as I like to cut a swell,
 I put up at McClure's Hotel.

Where all great minds do gravitate
 To regulate affairs of state.
And too, there's other reasons why
 My aspirations are so high;
'Tis so convenient when is scor'd
 A bill against you for your board,
You can, by stepping down below
 (If you are aufait on the blow),

Persuade the Raynold Bros. to
 Accept your little I.O.U.
On which you'll get the scads to pay
 Your board and bills from day to day.
Or, if you're sick or cursed with bugs,
 You'll find below all sorts of drugs,
Where Dr. P. or Rob his clerk,
 Will serve you with a smile or smirk.

Governor Rudd wasn't the only one in Canon City to be overwhelmed with the three-story brick hotel. By 8:00 P.M. on opening night an enormous crowd of Canon City residents had gathered in the large double parlors and spacious halls. "Many took the opportunity to wander through the lengthy corridors and look over the arrangements of the building, and all agreed that the building was a model of its kind," recorded the *Canyon City Weekly Record.*

Those who hadn't been invited to the opening drove by the hotel in their carriages to see the spectacle. "At an early hour the building was illuminated and a brilliant scene was presented to the beholder," continued the *Record*. "It could be seen from afar and was gazed upon by the beholder with admiration. Many children gazed in wonder at the lighted building; having never seen a sight of that character, having been raised on the frontier."

Instigator of all the wonder that night was William H. McClure, civic leader and builder, who erected the hotel after failing to interest anyone else in the enterprise. McClure began his hotel in 1872, and it opened two years later. In mid-1873, the *Canon City Times* reported the progress of the hotel, calling it "a first class resort for the many invalids who will come here to enjoy our healthful climate and quaff the invigorating waters of our mineral springs, as well as to the capitalist seeking investments, and the tourist and pleasure seeker in search of recreation."

A builder by profession, McClure chose a practical plan for his hotel and top materials with which to construct it. The first floor of the three-story hotel contained a spacious lobby with a paneled oak stairway and a large, formal dining room. The corner room at Fourth and Main was occupied by the Fremont County Bank, and a room at one end of the first floor housed the drugstore, operated by Dr. J. L. Prentiss, who shortly after the McClure opening built his own hotel at the Royal Gorge Hot Springs. Expensive guest rooms and suites were on the second floor along with two parlors, one for general use, the other for special parties, while the ordinary guest rooms for everyday travelers were on the third. The basement, reached by an outside entrance, contained a barbershop, paint store, and hardware emporium.

The hotel, leased by McClure at its opening to Mrs. M. M. Sheets, a widow and schoolteacher, was an immediate success. Celebrities from all over the state and outside it as well stayed at the McClure House and praised its board and bed. Captain J. J. Lambert of the *Pueblo Chieftain* reported in 1875, "This hotel is the pride of the community, as it may well be, for it is equal to any hotel in Colorado in point of comfort and all that goes to make hotel life pleasant and agreeable. . . . The McClure House is one of the best in Colorado."

Governor Rudd, who praised the McClure House so poetically at its opening-night gala, was not the only "state chief executive" to be entertained in the hotel. Governor John L. Routt, staying at the hotel while in town to install a new penitentiary warden, was serenaded at the McClure by the Canon City band. At the end of the concert, according to the *Record,* the Governor "graciously came out on the McClure House platform and greeted each member in cordial fashion."

Actor Tom O'Malley and his wife stopped at the McClure in 1880 for what O'Malley called an "over Sunday stay," that lasted much longer. He remarked in his notes, which he had intended to turn into a newspaper article, that the red carpeting on the stairs, the rich draperies, and the carved and upholstered furniture dressed up each parlor like a "good stage set."

> Ladies among the guests dressed handsomely and all day you could hear silks rustling up or down the staircases. Mrs. O'Malley had a golden brown silk dress trimmed with seal brown silk fringe she had thought very fine, but was quite put in the shade by the very dressy ladies at the hotel.

Twenty years after it was built, the McClure House was sold to an English syndicate probably backed by the Earl of Strathmore since it changed the hotel's name to the "Strathmore."

The Englishmen soon leased their hotel to Walter J. Jones, who claimed he was the one who introduced oysters to the West. Jones considered himself an epicurean and when asked about his quail on toast, replied in a newspaper interview that he would rather "shine in al la de la cream la mode, fricassee and other like French and American preparations than be President."

Jones brought not only a gourmet touch to the hotel but four carloads—$12,000 worth—of furniture. The *Denver Times* called it "mightily well selected, showing the good taste of an artist, as

39

also the unmistakable ambition to be strictly up with the times."
Among the newly purchased pieces were a $600 Chickering grand
piano, iron bedsteads, brightly colored Wilton and Axminster
carpets, Point, Arabic, and Brussels lace curtains, and a profusion
of bric-a-brac.

Today some pieces from that $12,000 carload of furniture still
decorate the Strathmore, but the "al la de la" atmosphere is gone.
The only rustle of silks is in the imaginations of the salesmen who
stay there or of Canon City's senior citizens who make the Strathmore their home.

"And as I like to cut a swell, I put up at McClure's Hotel." (*Denver
Public Library Western Collection*).

Little glamour remains at the McClure, today known as the Strathmore.

10. A Buxom Matron and Black-eyed Beauties
(Ore Bucket)

Breckenridge never did lack for a good hotel. As far back as 1868, Samuel Bowles was noting slyly in his guidebook *In Parks and Mountains of Colorado,* "There is a good hotel here, of logs to be sure, with a broad, buxom matron, and black-eyed beauties of daughters."

Early there was the Arlington Hotel, a fine gingerbread structure, two story with first- and second-floor verandas, and a double-deck outhouse out back by the Blue River. Just down Main Street from the Arlington was the Denver, another decorative wooden hotel. Then, up on French Street, just two houses away from the red and green home of Breckenridge's well-loved madam, was the Brown Hotel. Not lavish by Breckenridge standards, which were decidedly jaunty, the Brown was a good, serviceable hotel that

41

long established its dapper cohorts on Main Street.

Even the most avid Breckenridge historians can't recall just when the Brown Hotel was built. For years it was a private home and might have been constructed as a duplex since the building is divided into equal halves, upstairs and down, by a long front-to-back hall. If it were a two-family dwelling, the occupants used a communal hall and bath. During the early 1880's the Brown Hotel was occupied by Captain and Mrs. Ryan and their two young sons, and Mrs. Ryan conducted a school in the house. The Captain owned a mine, the Oro, and eventually he got tired of traveling back and forth to work so he built a home near the mine in French Gulch and moved his family to the new place.

Sometime later he sold the Oro—and possibly the house in Breckenridge—to the organizers of the Wellington Company, who changed the name of the mine to the Wellington and operated it as the best producing mine in the county for many years. (The last operating mine in Summit County, the Wellington was closed only in 1963.)

The charming house on French Street went the anonymous way of most mountain homes until, probably around the turn of the century, it was purchased by Tom Brown, who married a Breckenridge belle, Maude Mears, and opened the Brown Hotel.

Because of its long corridors and series of rooms that opened into the hall, the house was easily converted into a hotel. The decorative two-tone brown clapboard hostelry, with its fancy carved cornices and brackets outside, had a rounded entranceway which opened directly into the long hall that ended at the rear in stairs to the second floor. Overhead the corridor doubled back to the front of the building. To the right side of the hall on the first floor was the Victorian parlor with its hard sofas and ore specimens in a glass-doored bookcase. Behind the parlor was the dining room with a higher than waist-high wainscoting of pressed metal, and in back of that the kitchen.

Rooms on the other side of the hall were turned into the Browns' private apartments. Upstairs were nine bedrooms, the favorite above the kitchen since the hotel was heated only by an inadequate wood-burning stove in the parlor and the cozy cooking range in the kitchen. Everybody shared the bath at the end of the hall, and it didn't always work. One story tells that the Browns had the first bathtub in Summit County, and when the hotel first opened, people came from all over to spend the night just so they could bathe.

The Browns ran a fine hotel—Maude was a good manager, a friendly hostess—and soon the French Street hostelry was rivaling the bigger hotels on Main Street, particularly for the less transient trade. Many miners chose the Brown as a permanent residence, but though the hotel hosted a rougher element than the two others, it still was a "very respectable and self-respecting place . . . safe for maiden ladies."

In later years the hotel was run by another couple, Joe and Belle Marz, who kept up the Browns' appeal of comfortable rooms and good food. "They were just plain home-cooked meals," said a boarder, "but God they were good." There were hot rolls and pie with dinner, and for breakfast Joe Marz always made hot cakes.

Breckenridge slumped like the other mining towns—from 5,000 in the 1880's to around 250 over a period of fifty years—but there were always enough guests to fill the Brown Hotel. As the county seat, Breckenridge had frequent overnight guests on legal business. During the summers, the tourists came, too.

In the early 1960's, the the beginning of the Breckenridge ski boom, Guenther Hofeditz, an Austrian, a member of the famed World War II skiing 10th Mountain Division, and former publicity man for the Stan Kenton Band, purchased the old Brown Hotel, changed its name to the Ore Bucket, and began its restoration—not at a Victorian hotel but as a conglomeration of periods and styles which the Victorians would have loved.

The hall was papered above the wainscoting with a fancy, flocked red design. The parlor acquired a huge natural stone fireplace, a corner case of troops of toy soldiers and ironstone pieces, odd pictures, and a collection of iron implements. The dining

43

room was made into a bar. Most changed of all, the kitchen has walls covered with weathered wood, red gingham curtains, a rocker and a homemade shepherd's chair, copper pots on the wall, straw flowers, prints of mountain flowers, and tiny tile plaques. Hotel reservations are filed casually in a Cordova Cigar Company "Class" tin box on the kitchen table. The side of the first floor which previous owners reserved for their own use has been turned into a plush Victorian restaurant—the Parlour. Upstairs the rooms have been modernized, and the plumbing now works.

The favorite spot of Breckenridge skiers (they throw sleeping bags on the dining room floor if the rooms are full) who like to put their feet on the fireplace and sip glüvine or drink coffee near the kitchen fire, the Ore Bucket appeals, too, to non-skiing and summer tourists, who prefer to pass up the sterile pseudo-Swiss or gaudy modern hotels near by for the conglomerated charm of the Brown Hotel turned Ore Bucket.

The Brown Hotel, now the Ore Bucket.

The Arlington, at left (*above*), and the Denver, midway down the block, were more glamorous than Tom Brown's place (*Glenn L. Gebhardt*). Tom Brown built the first concrete building (*center*) in Breckenridge and used it for a combination garage and sign rest. Long before the current winter-sports boom, skiers (*below*) trooped to Breckenridge's hotels (*Denver Public Library Western Collection*).

11. It Ended the Night the State Went Dry
(Sheridan)

Theodore Roosevelt, Colorado's favorite visiting dignitary, never made it as far as the New Sheridan in Telluride, but the fancy-fine hotel gave a hell of a good welcome to another equally astute political traveler, William Jennings Bryan. During one of the silver-tongued orator's perennial political campaigns, Telluride's civic leaders built a fine wooden platform in front of the New Sheridan, decorated with red, white, and blue banners and American flags, so the popular politician could address the crowds.

The New Sheridan was only a few years old when it was chosen as Bryan's backdrop in 1903. As the orator could attest, it was one of the finest hostelries in the state that backed him solidly every time he ran for President.

Gus Brickson and Max Hippler, a Swede and a German, built the two-story New Sheridan, probably named after the Sheridan Mine, in 1895 and added a third story a few years later. The Sheridan wasn't much to look at from the street but made up for lack of exterior luster with a plush job of finishing inside. The lobby was a sprightly little room decorated with rich paneling and the finest collection of ore specimens outside the state capitol in Denver. A huge sofa was built into one wall, and above it was a library shelf for guests' use.

Directly behind the lobby was the mirror-lined American Room, the hotel dining room and sometime ballroom. High in a corner was a tiny brass-railed balcony which opened into the dining room and two rooms on the other side of the hotel. It was used as a musicians' gallery, and the players reached it by a slim brass stairway against the wall.

The Sheridan was known all over Colorado for its excellent cuisine which, it bragged, was the best in the state outside the Brown Palace. Anything available at the Denver hotel (Colorado establishments liked to use the Brown Palace as a point of comparison) could be obtained at the Sheridan—from vichyssoise to fresh strawberries, pork tenderloin and seafood to possum and plank steak—"two inches thick, a foot wide, and 'mebbe two feet long,' garnished in greens." A wine cellar supplied the beverages, and the hotel employed a Japanese cook to turn out pastries.

A street entrance in front of the hotel opened into the Sheridan's saloon with its calf wallpaper and cherry-wood bar decorated with carved lions' heads. Made in Austria, the bar had been freighted over the mountains to Telluride. A small area at the rear of the bar, separated from it by cherry paneling and leaded-glass windows, served as a gambling room. Behind it was the room which old-timers remember fondly as the Continental Room, whose purpose varies with each account.

The hotel today likes to intimate that the room, divided into sixteen booths, was the scene of illicit tête-à-têtes. Indeed, the area has its private back entrance, and its booths were once draped with sound-absorbing velvet-plush curtains. Each had its own plug for a telephone, and a special call board summoned a waiter when he was wanted—to prevent his over-solicitous interruptions.

But as scandalous as the Continental Room might have seemed, most old-timers say the idea that a man took his wife to dinner in the American Room, his mistress in the Continental, is nonsense. Whoever said that, declared a former waitress, "certainly did extort the truth. The Sheridan never allowed such goings on, and the waitresses had strict orders to be ladies at all times." Besides, said another, there were thirty-three saloons in Telluride, and anyone bent on indiscretion might well have taken a lady to one of them without bothering the Sheridan. Within the memory of most, the room always has been a coffee shop.

A simple, straight stairway separating the saloon and lobby sides of the hotel led to the second floor and the sleeping rooms. A third floor was added in 1899, when the *Denver Times* announced, the "New Sheridan is being topped out with a third story, and in sixty days that popular hostelry will throw twenty or twenty-five new rooms open to transient guests." The new floor was hooked onto the lower ones by the stairway, which just continued its upward slant so that the staircase was a long diagonal run from the front of the first floor directly to the rear of the third.

The hotel had been built with central heating, plumbing, and electricity. Several years before the Sheridan was constructed, a local mining magnate named Nunn gave George Westinghouse a reported $50,000 in gold to turn Telluride into the first town in the country lighted with alternating current. Though Westinghouse was long gone when the Sheridan was built, the hotel nevertheless was wired for electricity, probably by a local man.

Built far back in the San Juans, the Sheridan never entertained the troupes of celebrities that flocked to hotels in more accessible towns, but it did have its share of local high society. Bulkeley Wells, a gay blade and mine operator in charge of the Smuggler-Union Mine, was a close friend of Denver's social arbiter, Mrs. Crawford Hill, and frequently gave parties at the Sheridan for her and her friends. His favorites were costume balls, and to outfit his guests, Wells ordered several hundred costumes shipped to Telluride from Chicago especially for the events.

Sometime in the mid-1900's, heavy rains deluged the town of Telluride, causing a tremendous mudslide that ran down the mountain behind the Sheridan and flooded the hotel eight feet high with mud. The slide hit so suddenly that people weren't prepared for it, and one story tells that the muck rushed into the American Room picking up a table as a man sat behind it eating. For days the management of the Sheridan was cleaning mud from its walls and floors and finally had to use horses to scrape the lobby.

Greatly responsible for the New Sheridan's twenty-year success were J. A. and A. W. Segerberg, who owned the hotel for many years. In 1914 they built the opera house next door to the Sheridan, on the site of the Sheridan block, a building which had housed stores, offices, the Board of Trade, and the Telluride Club, until it had burned down a number of years before. Though called an opera house, the new building was more a vaudeville and movie house and dance hall than a legitimate theater. Special doorways were cut into the hotel dining room and lobby that led to the theater entrances, and room eighteen on the second floor was converted into a hallway connecting with the theater.

The dance hall–movie house was decorated with cut-glass chandeliers and private boxes surrounded with brass rails and velvet curtains. The screen, a Venetian scene, was painted by J. Ericksen, who also decorated the walls, designed the backdrops, and painted two pictures to be hung in the hotel lobby. The theater floor was flat, and the stage had storage space underneath so that when not used as a theater, the room, with its chairs shoved under the stage, was ideal for dancing.

The opera house had a short run. Like the hotel, it began its decline in the late 1910's. "The night the state went dry," remarked one old-timer sadly, referring to the Sheridan, "that was the end of it." The Segerbergs lost nearly everything they owned, and finally left Telluride, the little they possessed in a single suitcase. The theater was closed in 1925 and didn't open again for nearly forty years. The hotel was shut down intermittently.

Today much of the New Sheridan has been denuded (a latter-day owner traded its antique furnishings to Knott's Berry Farm in exchange for sterile, standard hotel furniture). But the owners hope that with increased tourist travel they will be able to restore the hotel to the grandeur of the time when the town's civic leaders chose it as Telluride's finest backdrop for Colorado's three-time choice as President of the United States.

Telluride's main street.

The New Sheridan about the time it opened in 1895 (*Library, State Historical Society of Colorado*). People in Telluride—and the rest of Colorado—were solidly behind William Jennings Bryan when he toured the mining camps. (*Denver Public Library Western Collection*).

A mud slide behind the hotel sent tons of muck down main street and through the New Sheridan Hotel.

12. The Best the Market Affords
(Cripple Creek Imperial)

Like the plays that attract thousands each summer to the Imperial Hotel's theater, the history of the Cripple Creek Imperial is filled with bits of strong melodrama. On the whole, the hotel's past is commonplace enough but spiced here and there with shades of innuendo and intrigue and just plain "good-will-out."

Built on the ashes of the 1896 Cripple Creek fire, the Imperial, originally two buildings connected by a passageway, first opened its hotel doors as the New Collins. Run by a widow, Mrs. M. E. Shoot, the hotel was described in an early-day booklet as having the best location in town, "being directly opposite the post office."

Though not the grandest hotel in the district nor even in the town, the New Collins was, however, highly respectable, thoroughly presentable, and downright nice. "Comfort is the description that fits every room in the house," declared a 1906 booklet entitled *Seeing Cripple Creek*. The hotel had close to seventy rooms fitted with electric lights and steam heat, thirty-nine of them in the north half of the hotel, since torn down. The lobby was fashionably festooned with floral paper, imported from England, in swirling colors of purple and red and blue. The dining room was Victorian proper with intimidating wallpaper above a wainscoting of pressed metal. Dining room capacity was supposed to be 150 though it sometimes seated up to twice as many guests.

The respectable widow Shoot operated the New Collins for several years until, unable to meet her mortgage, her banker, an English remittance man, foreclosed. The Englishman, George Long, moved his wife (a first cousin) and his young family to Cripple Creek to run the hotel for a while—but ended up operating it for forty years. Of noble descent, the Britisher with a monthly allotment from the Crown was anxious to turn the New Collins into a fancy yet thoroughly Victorian formal hotel, so he changed its name to the "Imperial" and filled its rooms with a boxcar load of fine furniture from Daniels & Fisher's Denver department store.

The Imperial under Mr. and Mrs. Long continued to operate as a respectable residence and tourist hotel. The couple sometimes entertained as many as 300 guests on days when the Wild Flower Express rambled its way up the tracks from Colorado Springs, stopping every so often to let passengers gather wild flowers. The Short Line narrow gauge arrived in time for luncheon in Cripple Creek, where Imperial limousines met guests and chauffered them to the hotel dining room.

Though an Englishman of impressive ancestry, Long was a quiet, gentle, wispy man who liked to care for the furnace and putter in the cellar where he kept a bottle of gin hidden in the coal bin. He was happy to let his likable wife run the hotel above. The couple was compatible enough, however, and ran the hotel successfully during the declining boom years, through the 1930 gold-mining revival to the deserted war years. After Long died in 1940, his wife continued to operate the Imperial, though at a loss, until 1944, when she closed the doors for the last time on the dilapidated, down-at-the-heels building and locked them against the past.

A couple of years later a young couple, anxious to settle in their newly discovered Cripple Creek, stumbled onto the deserted Imperial standing lonely and neglected beside a broken sidewalk. Shabby window shades hung in the dirty windows, and the lobby was bare of all but a battered roll-top desk and a potbelly stove. The kitchen was fitted only with a tiny, stained porcelain sink and a dirty cookstove. Undaunted by the decay, the couple, Dorothy and Wayne Mackin, purchased the bedraggled Imperial and began the tremendous task of remodeling and updating.

The Mackins attempted to operate the hotel on a year-around basis. Though summer business was encouraging, the desolate— and deserted—winter months ate up the meager profits. About the time the owners decided that to improve business they would have to find some attraction to draw people to Cripple Creek, they spotted a letter in an advice-to-the-lovelorn column in a Denver newspaper. Written by an acting group, the Pied Pipers, the letter bemoaned the lack of a good theater for melodrama performances in the state. The Mackins phoned the little group and invited them to perform at the Imperial. After only two shows, the Imperial proprietors decided to make melodrama a permanent part of the hotel's operation.

With the Imperial's success assured by the immediate popularity of the melodramas, the Mackins began the remodeling which they had visioned through the hotel's shabby-shaded windows several years before. The lobby, still bearing the lavish flowered English wallpaper, was furnished with a registration desk and box office built from parts of the furnishings of the original First National Bank building in Colorado Springs. Leaded-glass doors salvaged from Glockner Hospital in Colorado Springs were installed at the hotel entrance; stained-glass doors, also from Glockner Hospital, were put at the entrance to the dining room, refurnished in Victorian *décor*.

Installed in the Red Rooster Room, added several years later, was a bar that once served miners in the Red Rooster Saloon at Twin Lakes, Colorado. The Mackins found it in a chicken coop near where the Independence Pass resort had flourished. A photograph of a sprightly nude peering around a velvet curtain, entitled "Surprised," hung over the doorway of the Doctor Saloon in Cripple Creek before it was moved to the Red Rooster. Added in 1958, the Carlton Room, named for the late Mrs. A. E. Carlton, widow of a prominent Cripple Creek businessman, was furnished with a golden oak bar assembled from parts of three old Cripple Creek bars. The antique grand piano, inlaid with mother-of-pearl, had been imported years before from Germany.

With melodrama as the tail to wag the Imperial dog, the Mackins decided to turn the basement, a onetime gambling room and sometime Red Cross workshop, into a first-class theater—The Gold Bar Room Theater, completed in 1948. The room was decorated with old mining stock certificates, period photographs and paintings, and a piano whose stained-glass front came from a Cripple Creek parlor house.

Each year thousands of visitors from all over the world stay in the Imperial's Victorian rooms, eat at the lavish buffet, and cheer the hero at the nineteenth-century melodrama. From its inauspicious rebirth in 1946 to its overwhelming popularity today, the Cripple Creek Imperial is Colorado's most spirited old hotel.

The Imperial Hotel, Cripple Creek. "The finest melodramas in the state."

13. Well Supplied with Things to Cheer and Inebriate *(Teller House)*

"From an aesthetic viewpoint," wrote a critical appraiser of the newly completed Teller House to a friend, "the hotel is not a masterpiece of construction. Its exterior could easily be taken for a New England factory. Or cut off a story or two, it would pass for a cavalry barracks!"

Had the letter been made public at the time it was written, its author surely would have been lynched by indignant Central City citizens, led by the editor of the *Register,* who personally had been agitating for the hotel for more than four years. At least, the town's residents would have been greatly indignant toward the letter writer, and probably with cause; as much as ten years after it was built, the Teller House was still being called "the finest hotel in the state outside of Denver."

As early as December, 1868, two men had subscribed $3,000 toward building a first-class hotel in Central, and the town had begun a drive to raise the amount of $10,000. A year and a half later, with subscriptions only a few hundred dollars short, Henry M. Teller, president of the Colorado Central Railroad, which would shortly enter Central, offered to spent $30,000 on a fifty-room hotel if the community would pledge an additional $25,000. The result was a 150-room structure costing $104,000.

Construction began in July, 1871, when the *Register* announced, "Sluicing on the hotel site commenced yesterday with one pair of horses, one wagon, and one man. There seems to be some difficulty about getting the water in through the ditch." Excavation problems continued until a quick-witted workman directed water from a flash flood onto the hotel site and accomplished the work of several weeks in just three hours. After that, construction was speeded up considerably, but the hotel still wasn't ready for guests until the following summer.

Feeling personally responsible for Central City's hotel, the *Register* quite naturally devoted its entire front page to an article describing the structure. "The dimensions . . . we have forgotten if we ever knew them. But it don't matter. Our story can be made complete without a tape line."

The four-story brick hotel, whose front entrance was on the first floor and its back door on the fourth, was a simple building, in fact so downright plain that promenade balconies were later added to the second and third floors and an observation tower to the roof to dress up the New England factory.

The business office-lobby on the first floor contained a splendid collection of minerals and geological specimens of the Miners' and Mechanics' Institute. Adjoining the office were a reading room with a well-filled library and a barbershop.

The pride of the Teller House was its billiard room and bar, "well supplied with things to cheer and inebriate." Its walls were decorated with ten murals painted by Charles St. George Stanley, an Englishman who reportedly executed them in exchange for his board bill. The figures were heroic, among them Leda and her swan, Apollo, Venus with an apple, Libera and a wine glass, Diana, an armored Mars, Aphrodite, and Juno. Though painted in all seriousness, the murals emerged with a sense of humor: the goddess in one panel had only one breast; another figure was painted with two left feet, both headed in the opposite direction of the body. For a time the bar was called "The Elevator," after a sign, "To The Elevator," which some wag hung next to the barroom door, much to the indignation of unsuspecting women.

At least one hundred persons could be seated in the Teller House dining room, though on occasion the proprietors tried to "cram about two hundred people into it." A ladies' ordinary, seating thirty, adjoined it. The kitchen was furnished with the most modern equipment available, including an immense cooking range that "looks like a narrow gauge locomotive; has rooms and cubby holes, and little secret hiding places, enough to puzzle anybody but a first class cook."

The parlors, according to the *Register*, were "perfect marvels of elegance," elaborately furnished with the latest approved styles in walnut and damask and fine Brussels carpets. The sleeping rooms, the majority in suites, were "tastefully fitted up with all the essential conveniences . . . but without transoms, ventilation being obtained by adjustable windows. Each door is provided with a patent safety lock, which when once the key is turned inside, cannot by any possibility be unlocked from the outside. Guests may therefore lie down to peaceful slumbers, undisturbed by apprehensions of getting their heads blown off." John Evans personally had furnished the front suite at a reported cost of $20,000. Bathrooms, the *Register* noted cryptically, would be installed at a future date.

The grand-opening ball was held on June 27, 1872, but the *Register* gave it scant notice. "We should like to describe the scene at length, but we have had the house on our hands so long already the printers are [beginning] to swear." Fortunately someone else did record the opening festivities and the elegantly festooned Teller House, decorated with intricately molded confections— a replica of the hotel illuminated with Central Gas, a Colorado Central Railroad train with a carload of sweetmeats and coconut caramels. Fortified by an eight-course dinner that included entrees of saddle of antelope with clove sauce and Phillips sugar-cured ham with Mumm's champagne sauce and desserts of fancy cakes elaborately decorated—candy forget-me-nots on pink and blue icing; red, white, and blue flags on white; yellow daffodils on green —the two hundred guests danced until dawn.

Naturally the Teller House was an immediate success, catering to the elite group of travelers loosely collected under the title "the Teller House Crowd"—H. A. W. Tabor, of course; Walt Whitman; Prussian Count Adam Steinback; explorer Henry M. Stanley; and that intrepid explorer of the mining camps, President Ulysses S. Grant.

Ecstatic about the Presidential visit and eager to outdo the other mining towns on the First Executive's itinerary, the residents of Central City paved the Teller House walk not with gold, which was far too common in Central, but with $12,000 worth of silver bricks brought over the mountains from Caribou. Anxious to attend to every detail of the President's comfort, the Teller House wrote to the White House for a mold of the Presidential posterior in order to build a form-fitting chamber pot for his bedroom.

Not long after the President's memorable visit—which was marred only by a small boys' snowball bombardment as the honored guest crossed the silver bricks—the Teller House was offered as a lottery prize in a drawing promoted by the Catholics of Central City. Approved by Bishop J. P. Machebeuf, the lottery was promoted to raise funds to establish a home for invalids. Tickets sold for $5. Then Protestants objected to the drawing, declaring that it was morally wrong for a church to hold a lottery, so the Bishop withdrew his support, the lottery manager absconded with the ticket money, and the idea was abandoned.

The Tellers kept the hotel in the family for many years. Willard Teller bought it from his brother in 1883; later it reverted to Henry M. Teller's daughter and two sons. But by the time the younger Tellers inherited the hotel, Central City had become just another old mining town at the end of nowhere.

Central City had begun to decline about the turn of the century and might have stayed a deserted village if it hadn't been for a few enthusiastic people interested in Colorado and culture and a combination of the two. Led by two energetic women, the town turned itself into a theatrical and social center and inadvertently a tourist attraction. Eventually the Teller heirs sold the hotel to the Central City Opera Association, which could operate it in the grand manner of the 1870's.

Instead of merely decorating the hotel to emphasize its oldness, the Opera Association completely restored it, scraping off sometimes twelve layers of paint and paper on the walls. The original murals in the bar were repainted by a local artist; furniture long since junked was repaired; the second-floor dining room—a roost for chickens during the declining years—was redecorated and reopened. The Teller House even added a little current legend to linger with the old. In 1936 artist Herndon Davis painted a portrait of his wife on the floor of the old barroom. Mingled with the ballad poem, "The Face on the Barroom Floor," the painting now outdraws nearly all of Central's old relics as the town's leading tourist attraction.

The early-day Teller House, decorated with iron balconies to keep it from looking like a "New England factory." Among other delicacies, New Year's, 1873, dinner featured hump of buffalo calf, Rocky Mountain black bear, and Wm. Otterbach's Christmas Premium Loin of Beef.

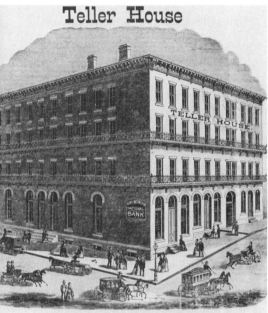

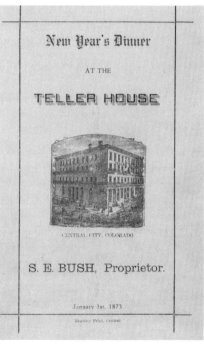

The Teller House lobby with its splendid collection of ore specimens (*Denver Public Library Western Collection*).

Murals on the barroom walls were originally painted by an Englishman in exchange for his board bill (*Library, State Historical Society of Colorado. Photograph by Charles F. Snow*). Central's most popular attraction today (*right*)—the face on the barroom floor.

14. France and Its Refinements
(Hotel de Paris)

"If this were my place," remarked a Frenchman surveying the splendid dining room of the Hotel de Paris, "oh, I would have slave girls and music at dessert; with my wines I would have the ceiling to open and orange blossoms and roses to fall upon the table."

"I," said Louis Dupuy, chef par excellence and proprietor, "make one smell the roses and imagine the slave girls by my wine."

Adolphe François Gerard by christening, Louis Dupuy by choice, "French Louie" by consent, the man who built the Hotel de Paris in Georgetown was a mysterious figure whose true identity was secret from all but his closest friends until his death. Nothing better described him than his obituary, written in 1900:

> Odder men than Louis Dupuy . . . never existed. Of a fine old French family, the descendant of heroes, he was a spendthrift, an emigre, a scholar and a cook and withal one who is mourned by the entire community for his great heart and ready sympathy. For Louis Dupuy . . .the gentleman, the student, the philosopher and the cook sans par, has brought a bit of France and its refinements into the granite slopes and rugged passes of Colorado.

Born into an illustrious French family named Gerard, Adolphe was intended for the priesthood but left the seminary for a career as an itinerant journalist and occasional cook. After dissipating a $50,000 inheritance, he left France for the United States in 1868 to join the cavalry. Eight months on a horse was enough for Adolphe Gerard, who deserted, changed his name to Louis Dupuy, and went to Denver to work as a *Rocky Mountain News* carrier. A few months later he wrote a letter to his employer, William H. Byers, chiding him for an article about France in the newspaper. The editor detected a literary knack in the young Frenchman and assigned him a beat covering the mining towns, which Dupuy gladly accepted. After a time as a journalist, Louis again deserted, this time to become a miner.

"French Louie" had spent only a short time in the Georgetown mines when he was seriously injured in an accident. Though he was not expected to recover, the miners took up a collection for Dupuy, and when he did mend, they presented him with the money, which he used to rent a bakery shop called Delmonico's. Somewhere Dupuy had learned to be an excellent cook and baker—a chef. Delmonico's reaped for its proprietor a tidy profit, which he spent turning the little bakeshop into a restaurant and eventually into a hotel—the unique Hotel de Paris.

Painted yellow and decorated with iron grillwork, the two-story Hotel de Paris (pronounced by all but Dupuy as "dee Pare'is") was decorated with a painting of the crossed flags of France and the United States, and above it, on the roof, was a statue of blind Justice with the inscription, *"Fiat Justitia Ruat Coelum."* (It was rumored that Dupuy had placed the statue there to chide the courthouse for not having a similar one.) On the other side of the hotel a stone lion crouched above a courtyard gate.

The little hotel, far more elegant than the provincial inn which Dupuy had at first intended, was filled with gaslights purchased from Tiffany's, pretty little marble sinks in each room, leather-covered books, oil paintings, and rare etchings. The drummers' room and sitting room, decorated with black walnut woodwork carved by a French craftsman named Gallet, was fitted with intricately designed beds that folded up to look like writing desks. The library (at his death Dupuy had 3,000 volumes in the hotel) was filled with books on philosophy, particularly the pessimistic thoughts that Dupuy adhered to, and furnished with leather tufted chairs, their arms carved with dogs' heads. The dining room had a yellow and brown striped floor made of alternating strips of walnut and maple, and a fountain, filled with mountain trout ready to be plucked out by the chef. Dupuy served his guests on flowered Haviland Limoges china, which he kept in a bow-front cupboard in the rear of the room. His own apartments were just off the dining room—a study lined with books, a sitting room, and a bathroom completely fitted in black walnut. Upstairs were ten bedrooms furnished in the most expensive styles of the 1870's. In the cellar was the wine room—without racks for bottles. Dupuy preferred to import casks of wine from France and bottle it himself as it was needed, and kept a supply of labels ready to paste on the containers.

The dilettante Dupuy was dressed in tails to welcome opening-night guests and show them around the Hotel de Paris. After a few introductory remarks, he excused himself—to have a word with the cook. A few minutes later he reappeared dressed in a starched white chef's costume and to his guests' delight prepared their dinners himself. "The time to see Dupuy," wrote a visitor once, "is when, seated at the table, you watch him cooking your order on a pure white porcelain stove."

Dupuy was indeed a fine chef, possibly the best of his time in Colorado, and he cooked not only for opening-night guests but for all hotel visitors during the twenty-five years he ran the Hotel de Paris. At the grand opening Dupuy heaped the Haviland china with mountain trout, ptarmigan, sage grouse, hearts of artichokes, and wild raspberry ice—a taste of what the hotel intended to offer in the future: fresh oysters, *pâté de fois gras,* truffles. Breakfast at the hotel usually consisted of an omelet and wild game; lunch, a bird and wine; and dinner, a clear soup, game or steak, one vegetable, an ice, and fruit or pastry. Though he served no liquor, Dupuy provided his guests with ale, porter, and French and Rhenish wines. Dinner was completed with a cup of Dupuy's famous coffee:

> That coffee from Dupuy's porcelain stove is another nector. . . .
> it is as pure as the snows that cap the neighboring peaks and when
> the lump of sugar saturated with cognac is suspended in tongs above
> the brown liquid and the blue flame sputters, leaps and gurgles into
> the cup, the finishing touch to an epicure's meal draws the comfort-
> able feeling of satisfied appetite without criticism, to the host who
> so admirably fills every want.

President Ulysses S. Grant, Baron de Rothschild, Prince de Join-ville, and scores of local millionaires and political figures were among the guests who ate Dupuy's gourmet dinners. Once a party composed of Jay Gould, Russell Sage, General Grenville Dodge, Sidney Dillon, and several others, whose collected wealth was estimated at several million dollars, arrived at the de Paris unexpectedly and to their delight found themselves served stuffed ptarmigan, venison, fresh French bread, French peas, and a champagne punch, with a selection of Roquefort, Camembert, and *bleu* cheeses.

Though he was praised by all the wealthy and influential men who visited the hotel, Dupuy's greatest compliment came from Dr. James E. Russell, a member of the University of Colorado faculty when he visited Georgetown, who later founded an academic field based on Dupuy's theories. Given the same grudging welcome which all Hotel de Paris guests received, Dr. Russell nevertheless was charmed by the Frenchman and delighted at one of the "daintiest meals" he had ever eaten. After dinner, Russell engaged the pedant Dupuy in a conversation on educational philosophy and sat enraptured while the Frenchman gave his theory that man was a machine for storing energy to be used through work. To keep the machine going, Dupuy emphasized, man needed fuel and had learned through experience just what fuel was best, "long before you damned professors cooked up theories about it—and there are a few specialists who knew the secret. I am one of the greatest in this country."

Dupuy's theories were Dr. Russell's introduction to the household arts and sciences to which he later devoted a large portion of his career at Columbia University's Teachers' College. For his part in the conversation that evening, Louis Dupuy was credited as the "father of domestic science in America."

Louis Dupuy, with his dogged attitude toward his guests and his disdain for nearly everyone he met, was a misogynist. Legend has it that he once was refused by a pretty Georgetown girl. Undoubtedly the pedantic Frenchman considered women nuisances, and he frequently turned them away from the hotel, claiming he was full for the night. When occasionally he did admit a woman to the de Paris, however, she would find wild flowers decorating her bedroom and dining room table. Dupuy's attitude apparently did not extend to little girls, for he regularly treated them to parties in the courtyard with wine and iced *petits fours*.

The only female whom Louis allowed to work in the hotel was an illiterate Frenchwoman, the widow of the wood carver Gallet, "Aunt" Sophie. A tiny, rotund woman who wore black dresses with white waist aprons, Aunt Sophie did most of the work around the hotel for a salary of $20 a month. She and Dupuy, different in all but origin, were inseparable friends.

Late in the 1890's, Louis Dupuy left Georgetown for France, possibly to claim a small inheritance. Shortly after he returned, the proprietor developed pneumonia from taking daily baths in ice-cold mountain water. As his fever worsened, Louis was confined to his bed, where in his weakened state he was persuaded by the fervent Aunt Sophie to give up his agnostic theories and be baptized a Catholic. Shortly afterward, aware that the end was near, Dupuy rallied, called for two bottles of his best imported French champagne, drank the contents, and died soon after. Louis left the hotel to the Frenchwoman, who lived only a year longer to enjoy it. They were buried side by side in the Georgetown cemetery.

An early-day set-up shot of the hotel. Originally, it appears, the building had no side entrance (*Library, State Historical Society of Colorado*).

Louis Dupuy's *pièce de résistance*, the Hotel de Paris dining room (*Library, State Historical Society of Colorado*).

15. The Finest in Southern Colorado (*Columbian*)

At a fork in the routes of the Santa Fe Trail, where the town of Trinidad winds along twisted red brick streets, the Columbian Hotel ponders the stately and savage history which it watched and helped make. The legendary Sister Blandina hurried along its rough board sidewalks on her way to civilize the unruly town. Madam May Phelps paraded by the Columbian, her latest imported Eastern "boarder" at her side and an entourage behind, window-shopping at the local stores while displaying a little merchandise herself. Herbert Hoover and his wife sipped tea on the second-floor balcony. Actor Douglas Fairbanks and wife Mary Pickford used the Columbian as a stopover on the way to their ranch hideaway. During the tense months of violence surrounding the Ludlow Massacre, the Columbian was host to uninvited militia leaders fighting Trinidad coal mine strikers.

The Columbian was built in 1878 as the Grand Union Hotel and Bank Block. Rumor has it that the original owner, John Conkie, lost the hotel in a poker game before the place even had opened its doors, and the hotel deed seems to bear out the theory. Conkie held the property only two years and transferred it to the second owner about the time of the grand opening.

The short-term owner Conkie built a hotel to long outlast its gambling builder-architect's stay on the premises. The outside of the building was natural red brick, now painted gray, with ivory limestone trim. There were high-crowned windows all around and cast-iron trim and balconies. Massive stone archways led to the terrazzo-floored lobby. Three stories high, the Columbian was designed to have four, but for some reason the top story never was added.

There were close to one hundred sleeping rooms in the Grand Union, furnished with brass beds and claw-foot tables and fitted with call bells. One bell summoned the porter, two ordered hot water for shaving, three called for coal and wood for the black iron stove. (Rooms later were centrally heated by steam piped from the near-by Schneider Brewery.) Ceilings in some rooms were as high as thirteen feet. Many were decorated with molded plaster and hammered metal in latticework designs with flowerpot borders and shell designs at the corners. Hall ceilings were a crisscross flower design.

Besides a large lobby, a formal dining room, and numerous small rooms, the first floor contained the saloon, worked in walnut and mahogany. Its bar was a massive piece, much of it carved, the rest fitted with leaded-glass panels. A frieze of colorful figures ran around the walls just below the ceiling, and some of its robust cupids, entwined with electric lights, were repeated on squares of the hammered-metal ceiling. Another piece of bar art was an enormous oil of nudes Love and Psyche painted "after Bouguereau," according to an identification plate. (The picture, long since removed, hangs covered with a sheet on the cellar stairway in the private home of a former owner.)

Whisky at the Grand Union bar sold for fifteen cents a shot, two for a quarter, and the price included free lunch. Ladies were not allowed in the bar; in fact, the Grand Union apparently didn't approve of its ladies drinking at all since it provided no spot, not even a wine room, for feminine imbibing.

A scene of lavish balls and luncheons, the second-floor ballroom was more sedate and more to the taste of women than the heavy saloon anyway. Besides the gilded hammered-metal ceilings, the ballroom had a striped dance floor made of alternating strips of dark walnut and white ash.

The Grand Union, which changed its name to "Columbian" in the mid-1890's in honor of the Columbian Exposition, was easily the most popular place in Trinidad for the famous as well as the infamous. The town's leading citizens rendezvoused in the ballroom and dining room while some of the more controversial ones, such as Bat Masterson and Doc Holliday, cut cards in the basement gambling room, one of the finest in Trinidad and supposed to be a square deal. A row of Italian marble washbasins, used jointly by gamblers and patrons of a barbershop across the hall, still stands in a near-by room.

Along with acting as the core of Trinidad social life both sedate and salacious, the Columbian was headquarters for traveling salesmen, the "knights-of-the-grip," who arrived daily by train. The hotel hired one-legged Jerry Trujillo, the only cab driver in town, to meet salesmen at the station and haul their eight to fifteen trunks apiece back to the hotel. "We always considered the knights-of-the-grip the bacon and eggs," said Mrs. Floyd Beauchamp, who along with her husband ran the Columbian for fifty years. The drummers opened their trunks for display in their hotel rooms and sold the local townspeople everything from fur coats to kitchen-ware.

In 1913, however, drummers as well as local people were routed from the hotel by the state militia brought to quell rioting coal miners who were attempting to strike. The Columbian Hotel, a re-luctant host to the militia, witnessed some of the bloodiest, most vicious events in Colorado history, which culminated in the Lud-low Massacre. During the battle between strikers and soldiers, the militiamen, many of them armed employees of mine owners, fired on a tent colony near Ludlow, Colorado, killing a number of women and children. "Remember Ludlow!" became the battle cry of the miners.

During the intense days of the strike, the Columbian became the "capitalistic" hotel, the residence for mine owners, their hench-men, and the militia. Just across the street, the Toltec Hotel housed unionists. The militia investigated guests and staff of the Colum-bian, got rid of those whom it thought suspicious, and gave the rest passes to get in and out of the hotel. Everyone in town was subject to an 11:00 P.M. curfew, but hotel guests occasionally forgot the deadline and had to furtively arouse proprietor Floyd Beauchamp to let them in through a basement back door.

Union officials frequently accused mine owners of hiding ma-chine guns on the Columbian roof ready to mow down milling miners in the streets, and to the consternation of hotel and guests, Union delegations were sent to make periodic checks throughout the hotel. To further arouse the militia, along with patrons and staff, striking miners marched around the hotel with sticks of dynamite singing, "Union forever! Union forever!"

When Mother Jones, the aged fighting female labor agitator, was arrested, mine officials locked her up in a Columbian room. Indignant wives of the miners, hearing of her captivity, marched through the hotel halls singing union songs and demanding to see the general in charge. A wary officer finally faced the women and listened to their tirade, until a desk clerk shooed them out. At a point when union–mine owner relationships reached a final frenzy, the commanding officer, General Chase, afraid to appear in the lobby, would ride the elevator to the lobby floor, stop it just below the thirteen-foot ceiling, and read his proclamations through the elevator's mesh cage.

The hateful events of the coal strike and their wake affected the town for many years, but they apparently left little taint on the Columbian. When the militia left, the hotel returned to business-as-usual. The doors once more were opened to the traveling public, which gave little thought to strikes and strikers and didn't much care that the Columbian had housed the militia.

Once more the Columbian hosted teas, formal luncheons, and lavish wedding banquets at which guests consumed "tubs of champagne." Drummers returned to the hotel, among them the local favorite, the Buster Brown shoeman who brought his midget and his dog Tige to perform on the hotel's front steps. Once again the miners spent their evenings in the bar and gambling room. So popular was the Columbian, in fact, that the hotel paid a man ten dollars a load to haul miners from Raton and Morley to its doors on Saturday nights.

Along with regular guests, celebrities returned to the Columbian. Herbert Hoover and his wife took the second-floor corner suite for a few days on their motor trip through Colorado. Tom Mix parked his big white Lincoln in the Columbian lot and his dazzling white-fringed buckskins in a hotel bedroom. Will Rogers and Wiley Post spent a night at the Columbian on their ill-fated flying trip to Alaska.

Spanish dancer Carola Goya registered for a Columbian room and woke the following morning to find that President Franklin Roosevelt had declared a bank holiday and she was stranded in Trinidad. Unable to cash a check, she found herself, her mother, her harpist, and her pianist at the Columbian's mercy. To add to her dilemma, she caught a serious case of flu. The hotel people nursed her back to health and held her hotel bill until the President opened the banks and she had the money to pay.

In appreciation of the Columbian's kindness, Carola Goya gave a dance concert in the lobby and invited all the residents of Trinidad. The townspeople stood several deep along the walls and on the stairway. A few even crowded into the elevator and ran it up a few feet for a view of the fiery dancer. Result of the concert, which was free to Trinidadians, of course, was an ecstatic audience which encouraged its friends to pack houses at later concerts in Pueblo and Denver.

The Columbian Hotel today, completely refurbished, still attracts salesmen, celebrities, and performing guests. Recently the National Steel Band from the island of Trinidad, appearing in Santa Fe, New Mexico, spotted the town of Trinidad, Colorado, on a road map and made a spur-of-the-moment decision to spend their Independence Day at the hotel. To celebrate the holiday and acknowledge the pleasant reception which they had received, the band gave an impromptu corner concert just outside the Columbian for the people of Trinidad.

The Grand Union Hotel was built in 1878 despite the "1880" under the eagle (*Library, State Historical Society of Colorado*).

58   TRINIDAD DIRECTORY.

Grand Union Hotel,

F. L. CASTEX, Proprietor.

RATES $3 TO $4 PER DAY.

The Finest Hotel in Southern Colorado.

···•Special Attention Given to the Commercial Trade.•···

Corner Main and Commercial Streets,

TRINIDAD,   -   -   COLO.

Cupids (*above*) entwined with electric lights, carved walnut, and leaded glass made the Columbian bar Trinidad's finest. The day the Columbian elevator (*below*) was installed. The Columbian today and much as it appeared when the militia took it over during the 1913 coal mine strikes.

16. Aspen's Greatest Monument *(Jerome)*

Opening of Hotel Jerome
Aspen's Palace Hotel is Dedicated
In a Blaze of Light and Music
Ball and Banquet
Aspen's Greatest Monument
Distinguished Guests in Shimmering
Silks and Gleaming Satins
A Great Success.

Where "sullen ignorance once did undisputed sway," at long last on a November night in 1889 "imperial genius now presides." It had been a long fight; the newspapers might well sit back and apotheosize.

For months the papers had prodded lax Aspen citizens to erect some kind of a decent hotel. "Our views on the subject are well understood," sighed the *Aspen Times Weekly*, "but we will again briefly point out the advantages that would follow in the wake of such an enterprise." The time was near when Aspen's hotel facilities would not be sufficient, the newspaper warned the people, and chided the Chamber of Commerce for not finding someone "who would be glad to embrace the unexcelled business opportunity that is offered here." After columns of cajoling, the Aspen papers finally did discover someone interested in building a hotel—Jerome B. Wheeler, an Easterner with heavy investments in Aspen mines.

Wheeler began construction on the hotel, which was to cost him $125,000, not to mention $40,000 for furnishings, in May, 1889, and work progressed quickly (too quickly, it turned out) since he offered the contractor a premium for every day he beat the projected completion date.

Three stories high (the hotel stationery showed a four-story building) the Hotel Jerome, characteristically named after its builder, was a marvel of grandeur that earned itself titles such as "the handsomest hotel on the Western Slope" and "Aspen's greatest monument." There were a lobby and reading room finished in polished oak with a marble tile floor, ladies' reception room, dining room, bar and billiard room, a greenhouse, ninety sleeping rooms, and fifteen baths. The Jerome, described by one as an "architectural extravagance," had electricity and steam heat, and to the excitement of its guests, an elevator operated by a series of hand-pulled ropes.

It was an excited, frankly awed crowd of Aspenites who crowded into the Jerome on opening night to attend the banquet and ball, "rivalling in luxurious splendor some of the festivals of the capitol of ancient Rome."

> Beautiful women whose smile would inspire men to glorious deeds, flitted like birds of paradise in their glorious plumage. . . . Slippered feet and forms clad in shimmering silk and laces rich enough to ransom a princess floated like the billows of the ocean in rapturious motion. Jewels, whose sparkling irridescence vied with the sunshine of electric light lent an additional languor. . . . Not in the storied days of the first empire, nor among the favored hosts of poetic Venice, not among the glitter and splendor of the czar's capital was a more sumptuous festival ever known . . . never before, and probably never again in the pages which registers the events of the silver metropolis, will such an epoch be noted.

Attending the lavish banquet in the ladies' ordinary, prepared by chef M. Fonseca "but recently arrived from Paris," were Mrs. Ben S. Phillips in an elegant black décolleté evening dress of black silk and mull with yellow trimmings and a diamond necklace, and Mrs. A. P. Mackey, dressed in a black fish-net costume, en train, trimmed with gold and decorated with diamond ornaments and natural flowers.

And flitting from partner to partner at the twenty-one-dance ball were Miss Ida Bixby in seafoam China silk with diamonds and pearls; Mrs. Polk, costumed in mahogany and white with magnificent emeralds; Miss Clara Pittman in a concert costume of old rose cashmere, brocaded black velvet lace, and jet trimmings as well as diamonds and emeralds; and columns of others just as magnificently gowned.

For all its elegance, the Hotel Jerome, Wheeler noted with dissatisfaction, had not been built to his specifications. Apparently the contractor had made changes without consulting Wheeler. For one thing, the contracting firm had used pressed brick in the building instead of the specified sand brick. The transoms had been altered from the original plan, and the wrong furnace was installed. (Reportedly it was so large that part of the lobby floor had to be ripped up and later relaid so that the furnace could be put into place.) At any rate, the contractor sued for his money; nobody, alas, recalls the outcome.

Wheeler kept his ill-built Hotel Jerome for nearly twenty-five years, then leased it to a onetime hotel bartender, Mansor S. Elisha, a Syrian who had started business in Aspen as a pencil vendor in the post office before working for the Jerome. A couple of years later Elisha purchased it for back taxes. The hotel never closed during the declining years; there were always enough salesmen and tourists to keep up a steady if not always flourishing business, and the local people gave a loyal patronage to the Jerome's combination bar and soda fountain, where they could guzzle milkshakes spiked with whisky, called the "Aspen Crud." It "went down smooth." Meals were fifty cents at the hotel, seventy-five on Sunday, but with the Sabbath meal the diner was serenaded by a lady who played the piano and violin.

By the late 1940's the lady with the violin was gone and so were the fifty-cent meals and the Aspen Crud, the hotel greenhouse and the hand-powered elevator (though the elevator's replacement wasn't much faster). Aspen had embarked on a second boom of lush years in which the tourist silver came faster than the ore from the mountain sides sixty years before. Aspen had been discovered by the skiers and by a culture-conscious set led by Walter P. Paepcke, who set up the Aspen Company (whose stock is held now mostly by the Aspen Institute) that among other things took out a twenty-five-year lease on the Hotel Jerome. The lessees completely revamped the Jerome, adding bathrooms and kitchens, refurbishing and redecorating the public rooms (many of them

75

were fitted with pieces from the Palmer House in Chicago), and painting the outside white.

Today the Jerome hosts a crowd not altogether different from the earlier Aspenites who crowded into the hotel on opening night. The diamonds and pearls and magnificent emeralds are still there, and so is the sophisticated air of lush living that makes the Jerome, despite competition from multimillion-dollar hotels and motels, the most touted place to stay in Aspen.

The Hotel Jerome as it looked from 1889 to the late 1940's (*Library, State Historical Society of Colorado*).

The current Jerome (*above*), painted blue and white. Much of the furniture in the refurbished rooms of the Jerome came from the Palmer House in Chicago.

17. Finest Finished in the Country
(Beaumont)

"Next stop Ouray, the toughest city in the mountains, where they hang men, women, and kids and roast strangers," yelled the brakeman to passengers on the Ouray railroad as it approached the rowdy little San Juan town.

Ouray was in sore need of refinement and a little bit of culture during the rough years of the 1880's. Though one of the richest little settlements in Colorado, it was late getting its share of the plush life which the gold brought early to other towns. As late as the mid-1880's, for instance, there wasn't a decent hotel in Ouray, and as for hotel dining rooms—well, a man had to bring along his own pat of butter if he expected to have anything to spread on his bread.

About that time Colonel Charles H. Nix, who had sold his Albany Hotel in Denver for a handsome $340,000, decided to change the Ouray hotel situation and put his Albany profit into an Ouray hostelry. Nix engaged architect O. Bulow to draw plans for his Victorian-fancy, cupola-cornered brick hotel, described as "for its size, the prettiest and most artistically arranged hotel in Colorado."

The Gothic-styled Beaumont with two fronts—the ladies' entrance on Fifth Avenue, the gentlemen's on Third Street—was built of brick from specially constructed brickyards, trimmed in stone, with tower gables and a mansard roof. The building was dominated by a Gothic tower, two stories higher than the original hotel, that rose above arched windows. Without its tower with the fine slate roof, the hotel would have been a simple, almost plain structure from the outside, but the adornment gave the Beaumont a real air of Victorian class. On top was a fancy weathervane decorated with "1886," the year the Beaumont was completed.

On the first floor were offices that housed, among other things, two banks—the Thatcher Brothers Miners' and Merchants' Bank at the corner, the First National Bank farther down on Third.

The grand rotunda of the hotel rose from the first floor to the third and was surrounded with balconies on the upper floors. Its walls were papered with a gold velours and lined with large and small pictures of local scenery. A grand oak stairway led halfway to the second floor then split with a staircase to each side.

The twenty-nine sleeping apartments and parlors on the second floor were grouped around a walkway which circled the rotunda. At one end of the floor was the main dining room and ballroom, "one of the neatest and tastiest in the state." It rose two stories and had three Roman windows and a cathedral glass skylight opposite an orchestra gallery. The finish throughout the room was hardwood, the wainscoting and ceiling relieved by gold. Fifty six-teen-candle power alternating-current lamps lighted the room, probably installed by George Westinghouse when he wired the hotel. (Contrary to local legend, Ouray was wired for electricity by Westinghouse, not by Thomas Edison. (The Beaumont was reportedly the first hotel in the country wired with alternating current.

The third floor contained twenty-four sleeping apartments, *en suite* and single, not finished until sometime after the hotel had opened. The Beaumont was fitted with bathrooms supplied with hot water from near-by mineral springs.

Visitors from Silverton, Durango, Telluride, and Montrose attended the formal opening, held on July 29, 1887. According to the *Solid Muldoon,* the dining room, "the finest finished in the country . . . was crowded with dancers until daylight, and the ordinary, in which were set the replenishing tables, was a busy scene of activity during the hours the hungry did justice to the bounteous spread."

Declared the *Muldoon,* "Altogether, the formal opening of the Beaumont was a most propitious one and augured well for the future of this already widely known house."

Opening-night employees were loaned to the hotel by Colonel Nix's good friend Potter Palmer of the Palmer House in Chicago, and several of them chose to stay on at the Beaumont instead of returning home, among them a pretty young maid. After a weekend of revelry at the hotel, shortly after the opening, her throat was cut by a jealous lover, and since then her ghost has walked the third-floor back balcony the first hour of every Monday.

As soon as the Beaumont had officially opened, the cream of Colorado's travelers gathered at its doors. Sarah Bernhardt, Madame Schumann-Heink, and Lily Langtry gave performances from the hotel balconies. In later days Theodore Roosevelt stopped at the Beaumont. Herbert Hoover, an engineer inspecting the San Juan mining district, was another hotel visitor. Probably the guest who caused the Beaumont its greatest consternation was King Leopold of Belgium. Traveling incognito, the King, who didn't fool anybody anyway, stayed at the Beaumont during his visit to Ouray to investigate his mining investments, supposedly in the Camp Bird Mine. While demonstrating the technique of European mountin-climbing on the hotel balcony, he lost his balance and plummeted to the Beaumont lobby—landing unhurt on a big sofa.

For years the Beaumont catered to Colorado's élite, but when they came more slowly to the little town tucked into the San Juans, more and more rooms were locked to gather dust. Over the years the hotel furniture disappeared—much of it was destroyed when the warehouse in which it was stored was razed by fire. Then post–World War II tourists descended on Ouray, and the Beaumont found itself suddenly in great demand. The hotel refurbished its rooms and rehung its original clock on the stairway. In addition, it opened a restaurant in one of the old banks, a bar in the other, and, possibly in the ladies' ordinary, that tourist favorite—the melodrama theater.

Today, though the Ouray train conductor (if there were a railroad going through Ouray) would yell a different greeting— men, women, and children are happily welcomed by the merchants who live with and for the tourist trade, and mere strangers are the salt of the earth in Ouray—it is still possible to capture some of the flavor of the high-living plush life of the Victorian West at the Beaumont Hotel.

W. H. Jackson photographed Ouray in 1886 (*top*), while the Beaumont was under construction; the Beaumont (*center*), at its height. (*Library, State Historical Society of Colorado*). The current Beaumont (*left*), painted and neoned for the tourists.

18. One Clean Meal and Three Square Sheets
(Strater)

Young Henry Strater had three strikes against him when he decided to build Durango's finest hotel: he was too young to qualify for a building permit, he was broke, and he lacked experience in the hotel business. But these things didn't bother the dauntless Strater. He lied about his age, borrowed from his relatives, and as for experience, he didn't need that anyway.

The Hotel Strater, built in 1882 with his relatives' money and an illegal building permit, was four stories of native red brick trimmed in carved white stone with a cupola at the corner. It had cost Strater's family $70,000.

The public rooms—lobby, parlors, basement saloon, and shops— were finely fitted in carved, heavily plushed Victorian furniture. Much of the floor was tile inlaid; the windows were draped in velvet. The barbershop was furnished with Spanish leather chairs, and in one corner stood a harp, stored there by a music student who performed at chamber music concerts in the hotel.

The guest rooms—often inhabited during the winter months by Durango families who found their own homes too cold for comfort—were furnished with the inevitable washbowl, pitcher, and chamber vessel. Each room had a wood-burning stove; a few boasted pianos. The Strater was built without plumbing, so guests' needs were taken care of by a three-story privy in back.

An 1892 account noted that the Strater had been built "at a time when it was not certain whether Durango was to remain a mining camp or become a metropolis. This display of their faith gave confidence to others and in a very great measure made Durango what it is today."

Shortly after the Strater was built, young Henry, acutely aware of his lack of management experience, decided to lease the hotel to H. L. Rice. Proud of the Strater and anxious to please even his youngest guests, Rice often gathered visiting children in the lobby and entertained them with adventure stories, but though the youngsters were entranced, Henry Strater was not, and the owner and the lessee quarreled over that and other matters. Thoroughly exasperated with Rice, Strater attempted to put him out of the hotel but found that he could not because of the lease. So, failing to evict him, Strater decided to run him out of business by building a competing hotel next door.

Adjoining the Strater, the Columbian Hotel, Strater's new venture, was two stories with a third added shortly after it was opened. Strater leased it immediately to C. E. Applegate. Apparently on its way to success, the new Columbian had barely begun to give Strater a run when Henry himself was ruined; he lost both his hotels in the panic of 1893.

After Strater left, the two hotels were joined into one and bought and sold regularly for a number of years. But though Strater management floundered, patronage flourished, and the hotel never lacked for business.

The Strater employed an assortment of Negro porters with such colorful names as Dynamite, Chain Lightning, and Titanic, and among other duties a porter occasionally was assigned to drive the gaily trimmed Strater tallyho to the depot to meet incoming trains. Carriage drivers for the various Durango hotels were required to stand behind a chalk-line drawn near the station and were not allowed to touch a passenger's baggage until he had crossed the line, so there was a great commotion among barkers to entice travelers to their various vehicles. To attract attention, the Strater manager purchased two dappled gray horses to pull the hotel tallyho and wrote a call for the hotel porter: "Strater Hotel—best place in town, three square meals a day and clean sheets every morning." But the porter wound up with, "Strater Hotel—best house in town. One clean meal and three square sheets every morning."

To the further consternation of the manager, Durangoans were so amused with the garbled version that they wrote their own:

> *Strater Hotel—best house in town,*
> *Come all you boys who've been around,*

Chamber maids you'll find at hand!
Best damn girlies in the land!
Press the annunciator and you get
All you want and more, you bet!

Despite the Strater's attempts to protect the virtue of its chambermaids, the girls were well known for their amiability toward male guests. The fourth-floor maids' quarters, dubbed "monkey hall," were strictly out of bounds to gentlemen visitors, who nevertheless frequently found their way to the rooms of agreeable girls. Occasionally when activity got too noisy on the fourth floor, the manager had to be called to calm things down. There was a saying in the Strater that when the manager took the stairs three at a time, "It was bed bugs or monkey hall."

Not only hotel guests but frequently local dandies made their way up the stairs to monkey hall. One evening when events on the fourth floor were in full sway, someone fired a shot, and the energetic guardian of the peace, followed by the Negro porter Enos, bounded up the stairs to find out what had happened. The shot apparently had been an accident, but it had frightened a pretty little dance-hall girl called "Kitty-in-Boots," who had thrown her arms around her paramour, a salesman, and wouldn't let go.

"Oh!" cried the gentleman, a family man, as hotel guests began pouring out into the corridors to join the commotion. "Take her away, Enos. I have a reputation. Think of my reputation." And from then on the man was known in Durango as "Reputation ———."

As the finest hotel in Durango, the Strater was particularly attractive to the town's social set, which frequently held dances in the hotel's rooms or entertained in the posh dining room. The *Durango Herald* regularly reported the Strater's social events in its columns, describing the activity as, "The cheery voices and din of carriage wheels told that all enjoyed the evening," or, "The viands were choice and the guests did full justice to the same." The dining room, a particular favorite with Durangoans, had a menu that featured a variety of dishes ranging from mountain trout baked "hunter's style" to grenadine of veal and queen fritters to English plum pudding with brandy sauce, but the favorite food was chicken, and the Strater kept a chicken run outside the kitchen and employed an Italian to "killa da chick."

Unlike many mountain hotels, the Strater never did deteriorate. A steady supply of traveling men took the place of the miners when gold and silver mining declined, and about the time the habits of the salesmen changed, the tourist discovered Durango, delighted to find such a jaunty bit of Americana as the Strater.

In due time, the Strater, which had been modernized as the years went by, was restored to its original Victorian charm. A new restaurant, designed as a gazebo, was added along with a tourist favorite, the melodrama. Rooms were refurbished with red and white mattress ticking for wallpaper and floor-length striped draperies, and fitted with refinished antiques. The lobby was refurnished with plush-covered Victorian furniture and lights from the old La Plata County courthouse. To the delight of the summer visitors who flock to the Durango area, the Strater has been remodeled to be as nearly as possible like the hotel which young Henry Strater built in 1882, though old-timers miss one obvious exclusion. No longer does the manager take the hotel stairs three at a time: monkey hall is only a lusty memory.

The Strater Hotel in the 1880's. The three-story brick building next to it was built as the competing Columbian Hotel (*Library, State Historical Society of Colorado*).

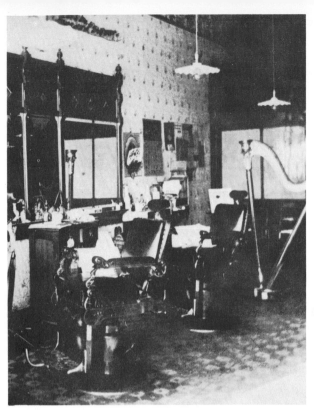

The barbershop was fitted with hand-tooled Spanish leather chairs. The harp in the corner was stored there temporarily by a music student. Presidential nominee John F. Kennedy spoke in the Strater's Gold Room during his 1960 campaign. The Strater Hotel as it appears to tourists today.

19. Home of the Silver Kings
(Silverton Imperial)

Silverton "hotels and restaurants are reaping a harvest, with
rates the same as the hotel palaces of Chicago or Denver,"
wrote the *Denver Tribune* in 1880 to knowing readers aware that
Silverton couldn't offer decent accommodations for any amount
of money. The town was long overdue for a first-class hotel, but it
took a visiting Englishman to do something about the situation.

W. S Thomson, a Londoner who had gone to Silverton to look
after his interests in the Martha Rose Smelter, saw the business
readily available to anyone who had the capital and courage to
construct a fine hotel in the raw, rowdy mining town of Silverton. So at a cost of $60,000 (much of which Thomson had made
in England supplying the royal family with perfume) the Englishman built the Thomson Block, known as the Grand Hotel, a
sturdy three-story building whose foundation was solid stone ma-
sonry. It was a pretty building, gracefully designed with French
plate-glass shop windows on the street, round-top windows on
the second floor, and a mansard roof with an American flag
flying on top.

Through the handsome entrance door, which was opened with
a knob bearing the state seal of Colorado, was the lobby, its woodwork painted chocolate and cream, its walls hung "with very
appropriate paintings." Just off the lobby, the dining room, which
seated one hundred, was decorated with a finish both "costly and
durable" and fitted with luxurious carpets and marble-topped
sideboards. It was described as "most excellently furnished and
presents an inviting appearance to the most fashionable and aristocratic guests."

Thomson spared "no pains or expense . . .to make this house
equal in comfort and convenience to the best hotels in the East"
and added the very finest furnishings to the lobby and first-floor
public rooms, which undoubtedly included a ladies' ordinary, par-

lors, and a saloon. The second floor had eighteen large rooms, among them the bridal chamber furnished in a "neat and tasty manner." The third-floor had thirty-eight additional sleeping rooms. In the entire hotel there were three bathrooms "easy of access . . . hot and cold running water is furnished." In the basement was a ballroom.

As soon as it was opened to the public in 1883, the Grand Hotel was the chosen favorite of Silverton's millionaires and came to be known as "the home of the silver kings." A hard-drinking, tough-fisted lot, they bypassed the fashionable lobby and the soft-carpeted dining room for the comfort of the Hub Saloon, the Grand Hotel's bar. Made especially for the Grand, the saloon's mahogany bar was shipped in three sections to the hotel on the D&RG narrow-gauge train. The three mirrors enclosed by the bar's massive archways were purchased in Paris by the French architect who designed the hotel.

The home of Silverton's bawdiest element as well as its wealthiest, the Hub never closed its doors nor locked its safe. (When one night a new bartender twirled the safe's tumbler, the saloon had to operate on borrowed cash until a man could be brought from Denver to figure out the forgotten combination.)

Silverton was a wide-open town and gambling was rampant, though some of the most interesting bets were made not at the gambling tables but informally, as dares. One dreary afternoon as a group of men sat around the bar at the Hub, one bet another that he couldn't climb 12,400-foot Mt. Kendall and be back in less than two hours. The second man took the dare, and as the others watched his progress through field glasses, he climbed the mountain and was back at the Hub in an hour and fifty minutes. Then after a few drinks, he bet he could better his own record, so he scaled the peak again and on the way down slipped and fell to his death.

The hotel management went to great lengths to entertain the hotel guests—such as enticing Lillian Russell, visiting the hotel with her escort Diamond Jim Brady, to perform—but no one ever pleased the townspeople like Hub manager Jack Slattery, who once hired major-league baseball players to perform in Silverton for his own entertainment.

(The Grand was not the only hotel in Silverton with a colorful management, however. "Cap" Walker, a former steamboat captain with the sweetest voice and the wickedest mind in Silverton, ran the Walker House, a fairly respectable boardinghouse. When a boarder of his who owed him quite a bit of money died, some friends of the Captain's tried to sympathize with him over the loss, but Walker replied, "Well, I guess I charged him too much; if I hadn't charged him so much, I wouldn't have lost so much.")

Renamed the "Imperial" and later the "Grand Imperial," the hotel was one of the first of the fine Colorado hotels to decline. When prohibition came, the hotel lost its best source of income and was hard put to find the money to stay open. The management changed frequently during those years, too. (One owner was Henry Frecker, who reportedly had deserted his family in Victor to become a hermit near Silverton. His daughter thought he was dead until she inherited the Grand nearly forty years after he disappeared.)

For many years the hotel led a precarious life. In 1950, Winfield Morton, president of the Texas Housing Company of Dallas, visiting in Silverton to check holdings, was smitten by the Grand-turned-Imperial-turned-Grand Imperial and returned the following summer to buy it. In nine months he spent $350,000 turning the $60,000 hotel's fifty-six rooms and three bathrooms into forty-two rooms with as many baths. The center core of the hotel, once used for jury rooms, was remodeled into a tier of inside rooms; the basement was divided into twenty inexpensive sleeping rooms.

Morton remodeled the entire hotel, but nowhere did he catch the flavor of old-time Silverton as well as in the Hub Saloon, where he covered the walls with antique beer advertisements— Coors, Silverton Brewery, Blue Ribbon beer and oysters, P. Schoenhofen Brewing Company, Lemp beer—needlepoint ships, Zubelda cigarette ads, robust nudes, and girlie pictures.

After spending nearly six times the Grand Imperial's original building cost just to refurbish the old hotel, Morton found that local taxes made the hotel far too expensive to operate, so the Grand Imperial was sold under a mortgage foreclosure and then sold again. Colorado Springs interests currently operate the hotel off profits derived from nostalgic tourists—noontime travelers on the D&RG Durango-Silverton narrow-gauge run or overnighters hooked on the decaying charms of the once fast and fashionable silver-mining town.

The Grand, Imperial, and Grand Imperial in Silverton.

20. The Best News in Many a Day
(Vendome)

"The house should have been opened months ago, had it not been for the foolish manner in which the Leadville Hotel Company conducted its affairs," declared the *Leadville Chronicle* indignantly. The newspaper had stated succinctly what many Leadville civic leaders had been muttering to one another for some time. Leadville had needed a first-class hotel for years, ever since the big gold discoveries had indicated that it would be an important city. The hastily constructed Clarendon Hotel was old fashioned and didn't appeal to the many Eastern investors who wanted to spend time in Leadville but who stayed away for lack of decent accommodations.

When a group of businessmen finally did organize in 1883, under the name of the Leadville Hotel Company, to build a first-class hostelry, they quibbled over details and haggled over money and finally discovered to their chagrin that they couldn't raise enough to finance the construction. So using the guise of civic pride, they appealed to Leadville's "mother lode," H. A. W. Tabor. The silver king, who already had begun to suspect that he had overextended himself a little, was reluctant to join the hotel venture until he was convinced that he alone stood between the hotel's success and failure. Reluctantly, he gave his promise and in return received 51 per cent of the hotel's stock along with the dubious honor of having the proposed building named for him.

Two years later the hotel finally opened. On June 20, 1885, the *Leadville Chronicle* reported, "The best news the *Chronicle* has had to announce to its readers in many a day, is the opening of the Tabor Grand Hotel."

The grand opening took place a month later, July 17, 1885, when an anxious group of Leadville residents paid $5 apiece to nibble at a lavishly adorned banquet table and examine the $100,000 Tabor Grand.

The structure had 117 rooms, very elegantly appointed. The

rotunda, which was floored with colored tiles, had two massive walnut staircases leading to the upper floors and enormous circular
radiators to pour out the hotel's steam heat. To one side was a bar
adorned with a fancy wainscoting and intricate wallpaper. Cir-
cling the rotunda were a large waiting room for ladies, a library, a
public parlor, and the dining room. Designed to seat several hundred, the dining room was formally laid out with tables in pre-
cise rows, a sideboard at one end, and festooned pillars alternating
with lavish light fixtures. A wine cellar in the basement took care
of refreshment, and an enormous kitchen supplied gourmet fare.
So great were the demands of the dining room that the kitchen
employed a chef, a second cook, a fry cook, a dishwasher, a pan
washer, and a handyman.

The Tabor Grand Hotel stretched four stories into the Leadville
sky. A quarter of a block in size, it was built of brick with a mansard roof and corner cupola. The first-floor space on Harrison
Avenue was taken by several shops—a billiard parlor, a bar, a
barbershop, and a restaurant.

Leadville was thrilled with the hotel, and Tabor himself—either
so pleased with it or so anxious to get a return on his $50,000—
leased an entire side of the second floor for his personal use. A
hindsight view of the Tabor Grand, however, in a 1928 booklet
which intended to emphasize a refurbishing that year, suggested
a less than magnificent view of the early Tabor Grand. The booklet declared that the hotel was

> . . . a substantially built structure, its long narrow windows looking
> down on Leadville's main thorofare; a huge porch and wooden side-
> walk supporting a hitching rack along which ranged saddle horses,
> heavily-laden mules, buck-boards and shays. A saloon on one side
> of the main entrance, a gambling den on the other. Around the
> smoke-filled lobby men are milling. . . . Everywhere is action fol-
> lowing in the wake of gold easily found and quickly disposed of.
> A stairway leads to the rooms above. Bare, plastered, dingy, lamp-
> lighted, with solid oak furnishings and the inevitable washstand
> with its bowl and pitcher.

Regardless of what the future would write about it, the Tabor Grand inspired great pride among Leadville residents and proved immensely popular with visitors, who no longer approached Leadville with trepidation about lodgings. The Leadville paper, praising the hotel, noted that its new lessee was Mrs. Hutchinson, former manager of the Clarendon, and announced, "Under such superior generalship, the Tabor Grand is bound to succeed."

Soon travel guides began listing the Vendome as the finest place to stay in Lake County. "This hotel is noted for three great characteristics: it is the most central and most convenient to the depot, it is ably and liberally run; and its tariff is most moderate—accommodations and splendid bill of fare considered." Another noted that the rooms, "beautifully fitted up and redecorated," were three to four dollars a night.

The Tabor Grand was as great an attraction to Leadville residents as to out-of-town guests, and the local people frequented the dining room or bar and sometimes rented the upstairs rooms for private purposes. A particular attraction, as far as Leadville people were concerned, was the hotel's saloon and its proprietor, Powder House Billy.

Despite the boisterous, hard-drinking atmosphere of Leadville, the town had its share of temperance cranks. Their favorite trick was to walk into a bar, order several drinks, then after gulping them down refuse to pay. When one of these anti-saloon drinkers pulled the stunt on Powder House Billy, the bartender promptly came out from behind the bar and knocked the man cold, remarking that he didn't want to encourage intemperance.

In 1887 the Tabor Grand was acquired by the Kitchen brothers, who named the hotel after themselves. Known for their fine food, the Kitchens were host to mining men, social organizations, private parties, and theatrical groups playing at the Tabor Opera House. But the brothers' greatest triumph, and the hotel's, too, came on a May morning in 1891 when the Kitchen Hotel played host to the "chief magistrate of the greatest government the sun ever shone upon," President Benjamin Harrison.

93

"Personality is sunk in patriotism, and only loyal inspirations are harbored," beamed the local newspaper on that historic day. The city had been beautifully decorated for the occasion, and "the Star-Spangled Banner floated proudly in the crisp morning air from hundreds of public buildings and private residences, and from the gallows frames and shaft houses of mines," but nowhere was a building more elegantly decorated than the Kitchen Hotel where the formal reception was to take place. Loaded with gifts from local admirers—silver bricks, flowers, souvenir spoons, mineral specimens, and photograph albums—the President and his entourage arrived in the Cloud City.

Not only President Harrison but a fleet of dignitaries made their way to the Kitchen: Mrs. Harrison, Postmaster General John Wanamaker, Commissioner of Agriculture Jeremiah Rusk, two United States marshals, railroad officials, stenographers, newspapermen, and personal friends as well as Colorado politicians.

The President and his party attended a lavish reception at the hotel, then the President greeted local admirers from a flag-be-draped scaffold in front of the hotel.

While the hotel was at its peak of prestige the Kitchen brothers sold the building to the Phillips Investment Company, which changed the name again, this time to the "Vendome." Though entertaining the Presidential party had been quite a coup for the Leadville hotel, it frequently hosted millionaires and well-known celebrities. Along with the famous, however, there were a few of the infamous who pulled their antics in the Vendome. Laura Evens, the well-known madam of Salida, Colorado, was just "one of the girls" when she lived in Leadville, but already she was known for her impudent ways. She convinced a wealthy Leadville gentleman to escort her through the Vendome and into the elevator. Then turning her charm on the elevator operator, she wiggled her way to the controls. After getting the car stuck between floors, she ran it up so fast that it nearly went through the roof.

With the 1893 repeal of the Sherman Silver Act, business began going bad in Leadville. A number of merchants closed their stores and moved elsewhere. As business folded and people drifted away. fewer travelers checked into the Vendome Hotel. About 1910 rumors began circulating in Leadville to the effect that the hotel would close. To quiet them, the *Leadville Herald Democrat* sent a reporter to interview the manager, C. C. Cooper. According to the account, the manager

> ... came out flat footed in a statement denying positively that the place was to close anytime in the near future. "We will continue to run the Vendome if we have but one man to feed in our dining room, and if we have but one room occupied upstairs. But," he added smilingly, "I don't think we are in danger of having our guests cut down to that limited number, do you?" And he glanced meaningly at the register.

That "flat-footed" statement was more accurate than Cooper imagined because the Vendome never did close, not even for remodeling. It was sold again, of course, and successive owners refurbished and redecorated it and at some time painted the outside pink, so that today the Vendome bears little resemblance to the original Tabor Grand. The 1928 booklet demeaning the hotel's early days may not have been quite fair in its view of the past; however, it aptly portrayed the future when it wrote that little was left of the original *décor* but that "the atmosphere of those by-gone days still remains."

The Tabor Grand Hotel shortly before it opened, from a W. H. Jackson negative. (*Library, State Historical Society of Colorado*).

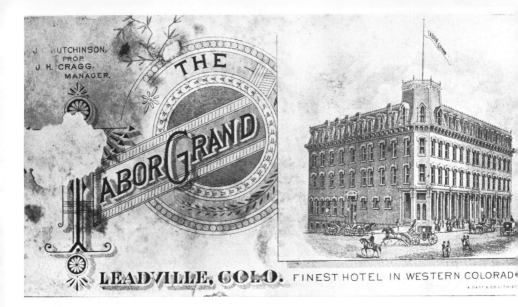

THE TABOR GRAND

LEADVILLE, COLO. FINEST HOTEL IN WESTERN COLORAD

Baby Doe's water-stained scrapbooks contained a card advertising the Tabor Grand (*above*). In 1891, President Benjamin Harrison, hands behind back, greeted Leadville from a platform in front of the hotel, by now called the Kitchen. Pointing to the immense silver seal is L. M. Goddard, who gave the welcoming address.

By the mid–1890's the hotel had changed its name to the Vendome and had hired a coach to meet incoming trains (*Denver Public Library Western Collection*). Except for the shell, today's Vendome bears little resemblance to the original Tabor Grand.

21. The West's Most Fabled Hostelry
(Windsor)

If the history of Greece is told in its monuments, Gene Fowler once wrote, then that of the United States is in its hotels. And of the most fabled hostelries of the West, the Windsor Hotel in Denver, he insisted, was the grandest of them all. The Windsor was a derelict when Fowler knew it best, but its past already was Colorado legend—the seven miles of yard-wide Brussels carpets, a gold-plated bathtub, furniture patterned after the paraphernalia of Windsor Castle, a specially constructed ballroom floor that cost $50,000. There was a block-long tunnel from the Windsor to the city horsecar barns, another to the Turkish, Russian, and Roman baths across the street.

Calamity Jane shot four holes in the Windsor's wall when the saloonkeeper told her that he wouldn't serve a lady at the bar. Eugene Field reportedly swapped the original copy of one of his poems, probably "Wynken, Blynken, and Nod," for a taste of the Windsor's whisky. Four Presidents and a host of poets and writers slept in the Windsor's lush rooms, serviced by a staff that included young Carl Sandburg.

The idea for the Windsor came from James Duff, representative of an English investment company, an indomitable Scotsman, who resented paying the outrageous prices charged for pitcher-and-bowl rooms in early Denver. An excellent enterprise, he recommended to his English company, would be a comfortable family hotel, a conservative brownstone with a little café in front, that could be built and furnished for $500,000.

Duff's firm liked the idea and under the name of Denver Mansion Company, Ltd., decided to erect a Denver hotel—with a few changes in Duff's plans. The result, far from the simple brownstone, was the Windsor Hotel, grand as an English castle, fabled from New York to San Francisco.

The nine lots at Eighteenth and Larimer streets alone cost over $100,000. (Some accounts raise the figure to nearly $200,000.)

The building was erected for $350,000. The furniture was purchased for $175,000.

Designed in 1879 by W. W. Boyington, a Chicago architect, the hotel was supposed to be a combination of the Windsor Castle in England and the Windsor Hotel in Montreal, Canada. It was constructed of lava stone from Castle Rock, Colorado, and trimmed with red sandstone from Fort Collins. Five stories high, the Windsor had a mansard roof decorated with iron fretwork. From the big tower at the corner of Eighteenth and Larimer flew the American flag; from two smaller towers flew the Windsor and English flags.

The simple, conservative company which James Duff represented found the Windsor too rich for its blood and leased the nearly completed hotel to three men, one of them Maxcy, H. A. W. Tabor's son, and the trio turned the Windsor into one of the most elegant hostelries in the country. In addition to the lavish amount of money already spent, the three put $200,000 more into the hotel before opening it to the public.

The main entrance was on Larimer Street—seventeen feet wide; six men could walk abreast through it. (The ladies' entrance was on the Eighteenth Street side.) All entrances had iron portecocheres and stone lampposts with four burners each. The burly black walnut doors hung on hand-tooled, engraved brass hinges.

The lobby, which had a marble floor and a twenty-foot ceiling, was flanked by a ladies' reception room, reading room, clubroom, barbershop, eight stores, and a forty- by fifty-foot billiard room. Off the billiard room was a wine room where the state legislature could meet undisturbed.

The Windsor bar near the lobby was the favorite haunt of millionaires and mountebanks—the diamond-studded travelers famed as Eugene Field's "Windsor Hotel Crowd." The mahogany bar, studded with $3,000 worth of silver dollars, was kept by Harry Heye Tammen, later co-owner of the *Denver Post*. (Tammen was so fond of the Windsor that when he wintered his *Post* circuses in Denver many years later, he insisted that the whole troupe, including the freaks, be put up at the hotel.)

Though Tammen was successful head bartender at the Palmer House in Chicago when the Windsor lured him to Denver, he always admitted that his fortune was founded at the Windsor. Whenever a gold-flushed imbiber paid for his drink with a five-dollar gold piece, Tammen would throw it at the ceiling, claiming the management could keep the ones that stayed there; those that fell were his. Despite the thick-plush atmosphere of the Windsor, gravity always won out.

On opening day, the Windsor bar was stocked with ten brands of champagne, six brands of American still wines, eight clarets, four Bordeaux, four Burgundys, six sauternes, three sherrys, three madeiras, three ports, five hocks, and numerous brandies, ales, porter, beers, mineral waters, and cordials, along with a regular supply of hard liquor.

Three massive carpeted black walnut staircases (as well as three elevators) led to the second story, the "parlor floor." (One stairway, the Devil's Head Staircase, cast such a sinister shadow on the wall next to it that H. A. W. Tabor refused to use it.)

The pride of the parlor floor (the hotel as well) was the bridal chamber in the southeast corner, and that was where Tabor lived with his bride, Baby Doe. The windows were shuttered and draped in satin trimmed with old gold brocade and silk plush. Furniture was hand-carved walnut, and some pieces had cost as much as $500 each. To the hotel's elegant furnishings, Tabor had added gold-plated doorknobs and a gold-leaf bathtub.

In the corner of the apartment was a tiny balcony, and to amuse Baby Doe, Tabor would climb onto it and throw silver dollars to passers-by. (Later Theodore Roosevelt gave one of his fire-and-brimstone speeches from the same spot, and front-row seats reportedly cost twenty dollars each.)

An oft-repeated story of Tabor extravagance tells that when Baby Doe wanted to bathe, bellhops and maids were hired to carry buckets of water to the tub at a silver dollar a bucket. When she was finished, the troupe would dip out the water and throw it out the back door of the Windsor for another dollar a bucket. The Tabors did live on a grand scale, but the story is too lavish even for them; the Windsor had running water in all its bathrooms. Many years later when President William Howard Taft stayed in the Windsor, his huge frame got stuck while bathing in the same tub, and he had to call for help in getting out.

At the opposite end of the second floor from the bridal suite, past parlors and suites lavishly furnished with massive black walnut sets and platform rockers, were the main dining room and ballroom. The dining room, which had twenty-four black walnut tables and three elaborate chandeliers, served its guests dinner on monogrammed Haviland china, fine crystal, and Reed and Barton silver.

Charles W. Rowland, a friend of Chief Ouray, kept the tables supplied with antelope, elk, deer, and bear. Other hunters brought in sage grouse, prairie chicken, ptarmigan, quail, and duck. Denver boys caught frogs in Washington Park Lake and sold them to the hotel. Milch cows were imported from England for the Windsor farm (now the site of Windsor Gardens, a pre-retirement-age housing development.)

After dinner, guests would smoke cigars from the hotel's specially dampened tobacco room in the basement or dance in the ballroom on the $50,000 floor. Constructed of German walnut and white maple set in a striped pattern, the floor was built without nails; instead it was mounted on cables in order to give resilience.

The third, fourth, and fifth floors contained sitting and sleeping rooms—in all there were 35 parlors and 150 bedrooms—fitted with a total of 1,900 towels, 100 dozen wash cloths, 800 sheets, and 800 pairs of blankets.

Across the alley was the "Little Windsor" with fifty rooms for female help. Across Eighteenth Street, the Barclay Block housed the baths, built of fine marble, polished hardwood, and stained glass. There were a sudatorium, shampooers' hall, plunge, cooling room, and several kinds of baths. Bathers reached the Barclay

Block by means of a tunnel connecting with the Windsor base-ment. (Before the Colorado capitol was built, legislators meeting in the upstairs rooms of the Barclay Block used the tunnel to travel unseen from the street to the Windsor bar.)

Four presidents—Ulysses S. Grant, Grover Cleveland, William Howard Taft, and Theodore Roosevelt—stayed in the Windsor. Literary guests included Rudyard Kipling, Mark Twain, Robert W. Service, Robert Louis Stevenson, George Bernard Shaw, and Oscar Wilde. (When the Windsor was renovated in 1937, paper-hangers removed a number of layers of pastel-covered wallpaper decorated with lilies and sunflowers from Oscar Wilde's room, sub-stantiating the legend that the temperamental Wilde insisted on changing wallpaper as often as he changed his mood.)

The Windsor hosted not only the most fascinating people of its time but the most glittering events as well. For more than a decade the Denver social season opened with a charity ball at the Windsor. Baron von Richthofen frequently gave dinners at the Windsor. James Duff hosted a St. Valentine's Day stag dinner at which the hand-painted gold satin menus listed fresh oysters (shipped 1,700 miles from the Atlantic), guava jelly, and prairie chicken. The Rho Zeta Club, organized by forty eligible beaux, held four or five dances each winter on the Windsor's suspended ballroom floor. (A girl who sat out a Rho Zeta dance in a parlor risked her reputation.)

The Windsor hosted concerts as well as social events. In 1908, for a Mary Garden concert, the hotel bought a Haines piano and had the keys specially rounded so that the singer wouldn't break her fingernails when she accompanied herself.

The Windsor's elegant years numbered nearly forty. By World War I, Denver had moved uptown, and Larimer Street found itself on the decline. After a losing battle to keep its high-class clientele (the Brown Palace had claimed not only the best customers but two of the Windsor's favorite managers as well), the Windsor finally opened its doors to derelicts. In 1922 the hotel was raided for gambling, and throughout prohibition it was soaked in bootleg.

During the depression years so many despondent down-and-outers hurled themselves over one of the old stair rails onto the marble floor of the lobby that the staircase came to be called "Suicide Stairway."

The first of several attempted restorations of the Windsor began in the late 1930's. The hotel was renovated, and artist Herndon Davis painted murals of famous Windsor guests on the barroom walls. In 1946, H. A. W. Tabor's granddaughter Persis, whose father Maxcy had been one of the Windsor's first managers, conducted tours through the hotel; later a melodrama was added; but none of these additions was sufficient to keep the old hotel alive. In 1958 the Windsor closed its doors, and a year later contents of the hotel were auctioned off—among them diamond-dust mirrors and rickety walnut shutters covered with sixteen layers of paint. Shortly afterward, with only token protests and little fanfare, the Windsor was torn down.

Like H. A. W. Tabor, who began his marriage in the Windsor bridal suite and ended it in poverty twenty years later in an obscure room on the third floor, the Windsor Hotel lived through Colorado's noblest, most brilliant years only to die derelict and destitute and nearly forgotten.

The Windsor Hotel, Denver, in an early-day artist's drawing (*Denver Public Library Western Collection*).

The Windsor as W. H. Jackson photographed it (*Library, State Historical Society of Colorado*). The lobby rose twenty feet and had a black and white marble floor. In later years the staircase, right, became known as "Suicide Stairway." The "Windsor Hotel Crowd" ate ptarmigan, quail, duck, frogs' legs, elk, bear, and antelope from monogrammed Haviland china in the fashionable dining room. The drawing room was only one in the maze of public and private sitting rooms which the Windsor maintained for its guests. (*Denver Public Library Western Collection*).

The Grand Rotunda.

Grand Dining Hall.

The Drawing Room.

Artist Herndon Davis embellished the Windsor's Tabor Room in later years with portraits (*above*) of early Colorado notables. H. A. W. Tabor, left, and Senator Ed Wolcott drank a final toast to the Windsor a few months before it was razed (*Duane Howell*).

22. A Peacock Among Mud Hens *(La Veta)*

The passing of the La Veta Hotel was a sort of commentary on its times. It was built by a village with great expectations for the future; it was razed by a town that never quite lived up to them. But for a while, the La Veta lived a peacock-proud existence.

The La Veta was completed in 1884 by Benjamin W. Lewis, who expected the hotel to be the finest between the East and the West. Certainly the people of Gunnison thought it was, and many a

Colorado traveler speaks nostalgically of the handsome old edifice.

Originally the hotel was to have been called the "Willard House" after the man who started the enterprise, but because of "financial embarrassment" Willard transferred the partially finished building to Lewis and his Lewis Hotel and Improvement Company. Gunnison responded by changing the hotel name, too, and called the not-quite-finished building the "Lewis House."

Linens, draperies, silver, lobby chairs, and even carpeting were ordered with an "LH" monogram. Then Lewis decided that he didn't want the place named for himself after all, so his staff was charged with finding a name to fit the initials. They decided on La Veta, the name of a near-by railroad pass, an appropriate title since the Spanish words meant "the vein" and the hostelry was intended to be a part of Gunnison's lifeblood.

The La Veta Hotel was impressive enough to merit the name. Built at a cost of more than $200,000 ($30,000 of the figure was for furniture), the La Veta was a four-story building with basement and garret, and took up a quarter of a block. It was pillared and posted, grilled and gilded, and capped on top with a mansard roof. There were wide galleries on the second and third stories.

Nearly all materials used in construction—the brick, the cast iron, the interior woodwork including the massive grand staircase —were manufactured in Gunnison. Most of the labor was local, too.

The first floor alone might have suggested to the hotel its self-imposed title of "the finest in Colorado." All rooms opened from the forty-by-sixty-foot rotunda, which had hammered-glass skylights and a commanding staircase, one of three in the hotel. Built for nearly $7,000, the staircase was black walnut, ash, and oak and was covered with corrugated brass plates. The newel, which had cost $300, was twenty feet high and two and one-half feet thick, and twelve men were required to put it into place. Steps were carpeted with fine Turkish rugs.

On the first floor were a bank with fireproof vault (it had eighteen boxes weighing 36,000 pounds, and the locks for them reportedly cost $2,000), a railroad ticket office, and a waiting room.

For gentlemen guests there were a billiard room with six tables, a bar (it featured a free lunch and the largest plate-glass mirror in Colorado), and a reading room separated from the two main entrances by plate-glass partitions. For women there were a parlor, a dining room, and an ordinary.

The second floor contained 40 sleeping rooms, many with marble mantels and washstands, a parlor with black walnut furniture, and the General Grant Suite. The suite's name actually was a pretentious misnomer since the General visited Gunnison long before the La Veta was built and consequently never stayed at the hotel. The third and fourth floors contained bedrooms and brought the total of sleeping rooms in the hotel to 107.

Besides the handsomely monogrammed black walnut furniture and the Turkish and Brussels carpeting, the La Veta boasted royal blue wool draperies bordered with blue silk rep and gold galloon. They were deeply scalloped and ornamented with long, heavy gold tassels.

The La Veta grand opening on May 22, 1884, was one of the biggest, plushiest events ever held on the Western 'Slope. A group of twenty-five experienced hotel personnel, including a crew of Negro waiters and a quartet of singers to entertain in the hotel parlors, was brought from Chicago to staff the La Veta. Over four hundred guests attended the opening ball sponsored by the local Masonic order. Both the Denver & Rio Grande and the South Park railways offered half-price excursion rates to those who wanted to attend the festivities.

The dining room was decorated with flags, bunting, and potted plants, and flowers and vines were twined around the columns of the rotunda. The dance program listed a grand march, quadrilles, lanciers, waltzes, schottisches, polkas, and galops. So grand was the event that for a while there were only two kinds of people in Gunnison—those who had attended the ball and those who had not.

Reporting the event, the local paper described forty-six gowns in detail and gave passing mention to the number of old wedding suits that had "come out strong." The most interesting account, however, was that of an out-of-town newspaper whose reporter described the high-style hotel as a "peacock among a lot of mud-hens."

Unfortunately, almost immediately the peacock was muddied with financial troubles, caused for the most part by a town that had started to decline even before the hotel opened. The La Veta was boarded up for lack of business during the winter of 1885–86, and though it opened in the spring, it closed again the following winter.

The hotel was sold for the first time in 1889. The next year the Ouray newspaper, the *Solid Muldoon,* advised railroad passengers to eat on the train since La Veta food was so poor.

Things rallied, of course (after all, the hotel was operated for nearly sixty years), and by 1910 the La Veta was considered a salesman's stopover. A magazine advertisement boasted "The Over-Sunday Headquarters for Drummers and Other Travelers."

In 1912 the Le Veta manager started the policy of serving free meals and providing free rooms to guests on days when the sun didn't shine in Gunnison. He kept a record in the La Veta lobby, and only twenty times in thirty years did the hotel have to pay.

By the 1940's not even the chance of a free dinner, however, could fill the old hotel, and on September 21, 1943, the La Veta, which had cost just under a quarter of a million dollars, was sold lock, stock, and grand stairway to a lone bidder for $8,350.

Today the hotel, degraded to a one-story apartment house, is a bedraggled resident in the Gunnison that grew up around it. The La Veta Hotel has become the mud hen among peacocks.

The La Veta Hotel, Gunnison, shortly before it opened (*Library, State Historical Society of Colorado*).

From 1912 on, guests were given a free meal or room for each day the sun didn't shine. Knocked down to a single story, the La Veta squats like a mud hen in a run-down section of town.

23. A Truly Remarkable House *(Grand)*

In beginning a description of this "truly remarkable house," wrote an enamored young reporter on the *Pueblo Chieftain* after attending opening-night ceremonies at the Grand Hotel, "the writer wished to be understood as speaking understandingly when he makes the bold statement that The Grand is a truly metropolitan hotel in all that the term implies, and IS UNSURPASSED UPON THE AMERICAN CONTINENT. We are thoroughly acquainted with the fact that articles of this character are read by many with a liberal degree of allowance, but we ask a full reading before you pass sentence in this instance, knowing that the statement we put in capital letters is true."

The ambitious writer, whose prose flowered through two and a half columns of type, had reason to be proud of Pueblo's finest hotel, which had opened the night before, September 3, 1887. Four stories high, surmounted by cupolas rising from the center and ends of the front and rear walls, the hotel resembled in style the Vendome in Leadville, the Beaumont in Ouray, and the Windsor in Denver. Like them the Grand had lavish parlors, dining halls, and reception rooms along with one hundred "capacious chambers."

The grandest part of the Grand was its rotunda, whose glory rose four stories to a roof of multicolored cathedral glass. "Even when the sun shines with its most severe mid-day ferocity, the intervention of the heavy glass softens and ameliorates its force to such an extent that the temperature and light are just what one desires." Around the roof the Grand thoughtfully provided escapes for smoke, dust, "foul air or any other impurity of a like character."

Tiling of the rotunda floor was not the " 'checkerboard' pattern of which the public have long since grown weary and tired," wrote the disdainful reporter, "but the dark and light shades are so interspersed as to make the floor in the words of a Boston lady look 'just right.' " In the center of that thoughtfully designed floor stood an eight-foot bouquet of cast-iron calla lilies fashioned into a fountain. In the pool of water at its base, surrounded by sea shells and tropical plants, swam a school of fish that could "sport and play at their sweet will." The effect of the fountain and its decorations not only was pleasing to the eye but added humidity to the dry air, though the ecstatic young writer did not speak of the result quite so cryptically. Rather he wrote, "Like breezes from off a crystal lake the freshened air is wafted through the rotunda and up the broad stairways."

The billiard room and bar, on the first floor, were fitted with tables and other furnishings by Brunswick and Balke. "It must, of necessity, be compared with the most magnificent bar in Colorado, and is for that reason unable to get a hearing," wrote the reporter. The "presiding genius," N. W. Clemons, was justly proud of the immense mirror, the finest fixtures and glassware, a $165 silver spice tray, and a silver punch bowl, gold lined and decorated.

The sleeping rooms, one hundred in number, were all handsomely decorated. "The Grand is the only hotel on this continent (we speak advisedly) where the top floor is furnished in the same style as the second," and where every parlor, sleeping room, and corridor was covered by either Wilton or Moquette carpets of the finest quality.

"Put a late arrival into the worst room in the house," the *Chieftain* man quoted a friend, "and he will wonder who the clerk took him for and why in the world he got the finest bedroom he ever occupied."

The dining rooms, ladies' ordinary, and clubroom for private dinners were described briefly, just as "so inviting that the worst dyspeptic will regain his appetite at The Grand."

His favorite part of the entire house, the reporter declared, was the servants' quarters, which were fully as good as any other portion. The sleeping apartments were elegantly furnished, the dining room "in no way inferior to those used by the public." The spread of silver, glassware, and china was "incomparable in extent and quality and the decoration creditable to the wares." Servants also had their own reading room.

In his adoration, the young man described every portion of the hotel. "The general toilet room and water closets, so often forgotten or neglected in many hotels have been objects of especial favor at the Grand." And later he wrote, "The water and sewage service, so often defective in many first class hotels, is perfect." In addition the Grand boasted, through its enamored writer, automatic fire alarms, steam heat, elevators, laundry, and carriage service.

The Grand was a Pueblo hotel, built with Pueblo capital and owned by Pueblo men. It was furnished by local merchants. The carpets and furniture came from Hard & Overton, who had had everything manufactured especially for the hotel. Burdish & Otero supplied silverware, and the Pueblo Hardware Company furnished "what was needed in their line." "The decorations in the Grand beggar description," sighed the writer, but of course that didn't stop him from elaborating on them.

"The writer cannot but feel his shortcomings in attempting a notice of this hotel," concluded the *Chieftain* reporter, "for it cannot be called a description for much of it is not even touched. It is an honor to the grand city of Pueblo and as good a hotel as America affords."

Later writers apparently felt their shortcomings, too, for few wrote about the hotel after its opening and none in the grand manner of that first-night reporter. One later writer made a halfhearted attempt at lavish description, but he couldn't touch the *Chieftain* man: Rates were "$4 a day . . . considered reasonable for the comfort, ease, and satisfaction afforded, by beds and a cuisine to which special attention is given, and parlors, ordinary reception and club rooms, that are particularly attractive."

Most accounts were strictly news stories. A mention was made when the Grand changed its name to the "Imperial" and another when shortly afterward it changed it again to the "Congress," in honor of the National Irrigation Congress, whose 1910 convention was held in Pueblo. Some years later the Grand was refaced and remodeled, its cupolas flattened, and its Chicago pressed brick—which had cost $85 per thousand—covered with paint. In the late 1950's brief reports appeared announcing that the Grand would be torn down and its lots sold for $300,000, the same amount its builders had spent for construction and furnishings.

With a noticeable lack of concern, the Grand was torn down in 1961. Hopefully its literary lover at the *Chieftain* wasn't around.

The Grand Hotel (*above*), Pueblo, the year it opened (*Denver Public Library Western Collection. Photograph by R. M. Davis*). In the center of the Grand's rotunda was a cast-iron calla lily fountain in which fish could "sport and play at their sweet will." The hotel dining room (*bottom*) was designed to be "so inviting that the worst dyspeptic will regain his appetite." (*Library, State Historical Society of Colorado*).

24. Yet to Have Its First Paying Guest
(Antero)

Most hotels take a year or two to build, a few perhaps three. The Antero at Mount Princeton Hot Springs was unique; it opened its doors almost forty years to the day after construction was begun, and consequently, it was just about always behind time.

Fanny Bell Heywood and Augustus H. Phelps, two Chaffee County pioneers, formed a partnership in 1877 to build a resort hotel near the hot springs below Mount Princeton. The partners did little more than break ground on the enterprise before they sold it to the Mount Princeton Hot Springs Townsite and Improvement Company in 1888. Two years later, after the company had made some progress toward completing the hotel, Colonel Edward Prince, an Illinois man, saw the empty walls silhouetted against the Chalk Cliffs and formed a syndicate to put a roof over them. He negotiated with the Mount Princeton Company to purchase the unfinished building. Prince and his company worked on the hotel for several months and had nearly completed construction—they had finished three of the four stories—when Prince caught a near-fatal case of pneumonia. When he was well enough to travel, he was carried from the hotel to the railroad station and put on a train for Illinois. After he had recovered, Prince refused to have anything more to do with the hotel.

For thirteen years longer the hotel stood vacant, until in 1903 Prince sold it for $50,000. The lethargy that affected previous owners must have been included in the purchase price; the new owners left the hotel vacant and made no attempts to open it. About 1910 an observer noted, "Although our roaring gulch has now quieted down considerably, the Mount Princeton Hotel has yet to have its first paying guest." Nor was it destined to have him for several years to come. The hotel had more owners, though. From 1911 to 1915 the Antero was sold nearly once a year.

Then in 1915, J. C. Gafford, a coal mine owner, swapped his mining property for the Antero, sight unseen. Gafford, who thought he had gotten the best of the trade, wasn't so sure after visiting the hotel, but he shook off the apathy which the Antero produced, and two years later, in 1917, forty years after it was started, the Antero opened its doors to paying guests.

The hotel, Gafford claimed—and so did everyone in near-by Salida—was well worth the long wait. Though opened well into the twentieth century, the Antero Hotel had all the charm of the 1880's. Three stories high (nobody ever did put on the fourth), the Antero was a gaudy green and yellow "cracker box." Wide verandas encircled it on the first and second floors, and a cupola stood at each front corner of the mansard roof.

A full 125 feet across the front and nearly as deep, the Antero had 100 larger-than-average rooms, many with fireplaces, most with marble washbasins and copper bathtubs. The entire second floor of one wing was reserved for servants. The ballroom was immense, and near by was a stage for amateur theatricals. Meals were cooked on a thirty-foot coal range, and guests ate them with monogrammed silver on hotel china in an exclusive pattern called St. Elmo. The floors were hardwood covered with long stretches of carpet. Hardwood was used, too, in the paneling throughout much of the hotel. Further elegance showed in the stained-glass windows and solid oak stairways.

Just in back of the hotel were the Mount Princeton Springs— seven main pools and many smaller ones. A Buena Vista pamphlet claimed, "Marvelous cures have been affected through the means of the springs," which averaged 130° and were not supposed to smell or taste unpleasant. A small bathhouse, designed by architect Charles Thiele in the fashion of a European spa, was built directly over the springs—a problem to construct since workmen found it difficult to pour cement over warm, wet, shifting sands. The bathhouse contained fifteen rooms—dressing quarters and baths—and two pools as well as a dining room patterned in an elaborate design of rocks and logs.

Near the rear of the hotel was an outdoor swimming pool, designed so that guests could step from their rooms into the warm water. But following the lackadaisical pattern of the hotel's development, the pool never was filled with water.

After Gafford finally opened the Antero, the hotel was immensely popular and attracted so many wealthy guests that it was nicknamed "millionaires' playground." A fleet of limousines met trains in Buena Vista twice daily and brought back guests who came to the Antero not only to take the waters but to play tennis or golf. (The $15,000 nine-hole golf course was a menace to a neighboring farmer who complained that stray golf balls kept hitting his cows.)

The Antero's peak year was 1926, when the hotel handled its largest number of guests. Bands were hired from Kansas City to play for dancers who flocked to the Antero. Financially, however, the year was a flop since most of those guests were free-loading relatives of stockholders who cost more to take care of than they

The Antero Hotel, begun in 1877, was not completed until 1917 (*Glenn L. Gebhardt*).

brought in. A few years later the hotel began looking for a buyer and thought it had one in the Baker Hotel chain of Fort Worth and Dallas, Texas. The head of the chain visited the Antero with his wife and son and was so impressed with the building that he negotiated to buy it. Before a sales contract had been completed, the son, playing in front of the hotel, was bitten by a dog. Contrary to some stories, the boy did not die, but the strain on his parents was so great that they packed up, sales contract and all, and left for Texas, refusing to buy the hotel.

Eventually, of course, the hotel did sell, but it never again operated as it had in the mid–1920's. In 1950 a Texas construction man bought the Antero and razed it for its good hardwood. Instead of going down in a few hours or a few days, however, the hotel once again showed its stubborn streak. It took the wrecking crews five months to demolish the Antero.

The bathhouse and hotel at the height of their popularity in the mid–1920's (*Glenn L. Gebhardt*).

25. Finest West of the Big Muddy
(Granite)

The raw stone, stained-glass-bedecked Granite Hotel that borders Denver's skid row sweeps the fringes of the jumped claim which General Larimer turned into Denver City. It made little difference to General William Larimer, Jr., and his greedy party, who arrived at the Colorado camp late in 1858, that the site which they chose for their town already had been staked out. They moved in, named the place for Commanding Officer Denver at Fort Leavenworth, and built four cabins at the corners of what is now Fifteenth and Larimer. The General took the southwest cabin, a sixteen- by twenty-foot shanty with a dirt floor and dirt roof and a glass window hauled all the way from Leavenworth to Denver City. By the time the rightful owners of the property had taken their case to court, General Larimer was firmly ensconced in his log cabin, and nobody paid any attention to the decision against him.

The claim jumper's cabin didn't last long in the rapidly growing Denver City, and soon it was replaced with a finer structure, a two-story brick building. Several years later, when the General's end of Larimer Street had become a crack business location, W. M. and G. W. (later founder of Clayton College) Clayton built an elegant granite department store on the corner lot to house Denver's bustling M. J. McNamara Company.

"The finest store west of the Big Muddy" was an impressive Colorado stone building, the first story with pillars of gray granite, the rest of the facade in varicolored stone. Above the iron and glass store fronts were stained-glass windows representing various national emblems—the shamrock and the thistle, for instance.

Through the vestibule, floored with "M. J. McNamara & Co." inlaid in marble, was the store's main shop. Lorgnettes and arm-length gloves, ostrich plumes and satin slippers shimmered under the shine of McNamara's four electric lights. A handsome staircase with a black walnut rail and cherry-wood newel or a stylish wood and gilt steam-powered elevator enticed customers to more mundane buys on the upper floors.

Designed by architect John W. Roberts under the direction of the Claytons, the dry-goods store was "one of the finest and most substantial blocks west of Chicago, and an enduring monument to the faith and enterprise of these worthy capitalists."

McNamara was a "business man of the most sterling qualities," and the *Rocky Mountain News* boasted that he was "one of that numerous class of Denver merchants who have faith in the policy of printer's ink" and that his colossal advertisements appeared regularly in the *Republican* and *News*. His Fifteenth and Larimer location was " a little out of the way," but the tempting bargains which the enterprising merchant offered "resulted in the acquisition of a retail trade second to no house in Denver." Eventually the location proved "wholly inadequate," however, and McNamara moved his one-million-dollar business to the cottonwood-shrouded skating rink at Sixteenth and California. The department store, reorganized a few years later, became the Denver Dry Goods Company.

Though McNamara moved out of the granite building in 1889, he kept a warm spot for the old place. In 1892, when he and several other silver Democrats organized the Post Publishing Company to put out a paper called the *Evening Post,* they held their first meetings in the alley corner of the old dry-goods store (now the site of a smart antique shop). Almost immediately the little group moved uptown to Curtis Street, but the stodgy, already floundering paper didn't improve with the location. It made little impression on Denver until a day three years later when a Dutchman and a Frenchman purchased the lackluster sheet and emblazoned their bold red headlines across the city in the reorganized *Denver Post.*

By that time the old McNamara store had been turned into the Granite Building, an office block that stumbled along unpretentiously for a few years with only a flood to give it any glamour. When heavy Cherry Creek waters forced public officials out of the old city hall a block away, government offices were moved temporarily to the Granite Building and left their mark in the oak doors installed to connect the rooms on each side of the corridors.

In 1906 the office building became the "Granite Rooms," with the title upgraded a year later to "Granite Hotel." Early days of the old McNamara store as a hotel are obscure. It was a plain but probably respectable establishment until it was sold in the early 1920's to a couple of men named Hartson and Colvin. The establishment went through various vicissitudes under the new owners, but not long after they had taken it over, they sold the Granite Hotel to a no-nonsense hotel man named Berger, whose family ran it for forty years.

The Granite Hotel was never very fancy. Its guests were mostly railroad men, and the only person of "celebrity" status whom it ever hosted was Sue Bonney, the elderly lady who was a Leadville pal of Baby Doe's later years. She stayed at the Granite whenever she ventured to Denver.

Never much, even when it opened, the Granite was a decrepit, derelict old bunk and probably would have stayed that way had it not been caught up with the rest of its block in an exciting restoration project. The Granite Hotel, slated for an entire remodeling —room rearrangement, new entrance opening off the back of the building, complete remodeling—is scheduled to become one of Denver's most charming old hotels, the cornerstone of Larimer Square.

The Granite's façade, varicolored stone with iron store fronts and stained-glass windows (*Library, State Historical Society of Colorado*).

GRANITE HOTEL

The finest store west of the Big Muddy (*Denver Public Library Western Collection*). The Granite Hotel will now become the corner part of the Larimer Square project (*Langdown Morris, Architect*).

26. The Finest Hotel in the District
(National)

When the National Hotel in Cripple Creek opened its doors, it modestly titled itself "the finest hotel in the District." A newspaper account was more flattering and claimed that the building "is considered the finest hotel ever built in a mining camp." A magazine said that the hotel was "the largest and most up to date hostelry in the Great Gold Camps." And townspeople, who never had seen anything like it closer than Denver, bragged that it was the "Brown Palace of Cripple Creek."

Five stories high with a gabled penthouse on top, constructed of 100,000 pressed bricks hauled from Pueblo, and filled with the finest furnishings and fixtures available, the National was indeed a building to inspire civic pride. During the twenty years it was open, the hotel played host to most of the Colorado gold magnates as well as to senators, governors, and Cripple Creek's favorite president, Theodore Roosevelt.

The National was financed by W. K. Gillett, vice-president of the Midland Terminal Railroad, A. E. Carlton of the Colorado Trading and Transfer Company, and a group of associates, to "meet the demands of travel in the new Gold Fields."

Construction was begun in early 1896. Since the foundation had to be blasted out of solid rock, work progressed so slowly that only the basement was completed by the time of the April 25 and 29 fires and little damage resulted from the disaster. Copied after the Alamo Hotel in Colorado Springs, the building was supposed to cost $75,000, but by the time it was finished and furnished that price had nearly doubled.

The grand opening was held in October, 1896, and though only Colorado's most prominent citizens were invited to attend the banquet, all of Cripple Creek was asked to a housewarming and ball.

Festoons of colored lights were draped across the front of the hotel from the fifth-floor penthouse to the ground, especially for the opening. Flags flew from the windows, and a huge sign flashed "Welcome" in electric lights.

Just inside the vast limestone arches, the lobby was decorated with pots of ferns and American Beauty roses, and for the occasion the hotel had hired Professor Schreiber's stringed orchestra to play for guests. The lobby was filled with fine mahogany furniture, much of it inlaid with mother-of-pearl. Polychromes in gilt frames hung on the walls; there was one of the Midland Terminal's Mogul chugging up Ute Pass from tunnel eight, another of the "Wild Fower Special" waiting on the tracks in Upper Beaver Park while tourists gathered armfuls of columbine.

Just off the lobby, the formal dining room had been decorated for the opening-night banquet with large bowls of bronze and yellow crysanthemums alternating on the tables with crystal candelabra. Negro waiters in starched white jackets waited to serve guests. Ladies could visit at the small tables in the wine room and sip their sherry or cordial while the men gathered in the bar.

On opening night the bar was filled to capacity with gentlemen milling around on the black and white marble floor. Just at the height of the evening, Spencer Penrose, newly made millionaire and Cripple Creek *bon vivant,* and a companion burst through the door on horseback, rode up to the highly polished bar, and to the crowd's delight ordered "a couple of horses' necks."

The second, third, and fourth stories were filled with sleeping rooms, 150 in all, many of them suites with private baths and service bells. Millionaire W. S. Stratton had signed a fifty-year lease on the plush fourth-floor apartment to "show his faith in the future of the District." At Stratton's order the hotel had built the fireplace of sylvanite ore from one of his mines. Polychromes of his Independence, Washington, and Abe Lincoln mines were hung on the walls near by. Paneled in golden oak with French mirrors, the lavish bedroom caused one admiring opening-night viewer to compare it with the madam's bedroom at the Old Homestead. Stratton used his fine apartment very little, however. Local residents remember that he preferred to stay in an old shack near his mines whenever he was in the Creek and to use the National suite only for parties.

One of the hotel's builders, W. K. Gillett, originally had reserved the fifth-floor cupola as his own penthouse, but shortly afterward it was rented by a Cripple Creek saloon proprietor who turned it into a gambling room. Johnnie Nolan, whose own establishment was just a few blocks down Bennet from the National, made the penthouse the swankiest gambling room in town. One of the town's former newspaper boys, who peddled papers in the gambling room and usually lingered to watch the faro bank games until Nolan caught him and threw him out, recalled the time when a gold magnate strolled into the National gambling room and demanded haughtily, "What's the limit in this game?"

"The roof," answered Johnnie Nolan walking up behind him, "and if that ain't high enough, I'll pull it off."

After its lavish opening, the National settled down to live up to
its title as the finest in the district. With fifty-two trains a day
pulling into the Cripple Creek depot, guests were plentiful at the
hotel. The National gambling room was the finest in Cripple Creek,
the bar the most popular. Ladies liked to gather in the wine room
to gossip, or visit the second-floor parlor with their escorts and
listen to ragtime music.

Guy White, the local favorite on the piano, wrote a tune about
the town that gained wide popularity in the district. Entitled "Down
in Cripple Creek," the song had a line in it about the National:

> *All of the people way out in the East*
> *Think that everyone in Cripple Creek is none but a beast.*
> *Someone comes along with a broad-brimmed hat,*
> *And all of the Easterners, they step back,*
> *And as he passes along through the crowded street,*
> *You can hear them say he's from Cripple Creek.*
>
> *One said to the other, "I had a friend who was there.*
> *He asked me to send him railroad fare.*
> *He said he was picked, but it sure looked swell*
> *When he stepped in front of the National Hotel."*

Built at the height of the Cripple Creek boom, the National had
a few years of high living and then met hard times. It never grossed
what its builders expected, and a year to the day after it opened,
they sold it for $125,000. The sale price was at least $25,000 less
than the amount that the National had cost to build and furnish.
The sellers explained to a reporter on the *Denver Republican* that
the venture had been a successful one but that "the owners were
so heavily interested in other properties in the district that they
were willing to dispose of this property at the price it brought."

The National changed hands nearly every year after that. Each
issue of the Cripple Creek directory listed a different manager.
In 1900, T. J. Nott handled the hotel. In 1902, J. W. Murphy
had control. In 1903, James O'Brien managed the hotel. The next
year it was leased by Albert E. Willsher, who had had "varied ex-

perience," according to a newspaper article, in India, China, Australia, Japan, France, Russia, England, and the United States. After changing the name of the National's manager in each of its issues, the directory editor gave up and listed the hotel just as "under new management."

For a while the National tried to present itself as a health resort. A 1904 article in the *Cripple Creek Evening Star* claimed that the hotel "makes it possible for the refined tourist or the health-seeking individual to see the wonders of a mining camp and receive the benefits experienced by all invalids who remain in Cripple Creek a short time."

The National even let itself in for tragedy. A local ladies' man checked into the hotel with a young lady one evening. The man's wife, suspecting the affair, flounced up to the room, shot through the hotel door intending to hit her husband, and killed the woman. A second shot blinded the offending husband. Though she was tried for the murder of the female, the avenging wife was acquitted.

Shortly after that a hotel man named Frank Johannigmann took

The National Hotel, Cripple Creek, shortly after it opened (*Denver Public Library Western Collection*).

over management of the National; he handled the hotel from 1912 until it closed in 1918. He turned the hotel into a stopping place for drummers who could make use of the fine showrooms in the National's basement.

But the drummers alone couldn't keep the hotel open. Mine closings and a constantly dwindling population, along with complications of World War I, made the National too expensive to operate. High taxes made the hotel too costly even to remain standing, so in 1918, the owner tore down the hotel and shipped its remains to St. Louis, where they could be reused. Up to the last, however, the hotel held on; a 1918 advertisement, placed a short time before the place closed, still claimed that the National Hotel was "the only first class hotel in the district."

27. Playground for the Republic *(Antlers)*

When the very fashionable, very elegant lady of the 1880's, with skin the fragrant whiteness of white lilacs, Mrs. Forrester, the heroine of Willa Cather's *A Lost Lady,* looked for a spot to winter with her aging husband, she quite naturally chose the Antlers in Colorado Springs. There she sat languidly chatting with smartly gowned women, flirting discreetly with members of the Colorado Springs "Little Lunnon" set, and sipping old-fashioneds at sunset on the Antlers' west terrace.

The very posh Antlers had been built by Colorado Springs' founder General William Jackson Palmer in 1822 at a cost of $125,000. Designed by a Boston architect after English buildings, the hotel consisted of three stories of gray stone topped by two of wood, and was a fashionable garble of gables, turrets, towers, balconies, and porches iced with gay awnings. Among the seventy-five guest rooms with two baths on each floor, the hotel had billiard rooms, children's playrooms, fine dining rooms, parlors, reading rooms, and so on, all filled with Gothic furniture upholstered in leather. The bridal suite had its own bath and was decorated with blue Turcoman curtains and blue Wilton carpets.

General Palmer himself had named the hotel the "Antlers" since it had seemed a good place to display the deer and elk heads that a friend in Manitou Park kept sending him. Much to his dismay, the antlers soon became hat racks.

Though the Antlers was slow in starting (a year after it opened, the hotel found that it couldn't meet its mortgage, and the operation had to be placed under a trustee), the hotel nevertheless soon became the popular vacation resort of Colorado. It attracted guests from all over the world, particularly from Britain since Colorado Springs had a prominent English colony.

The old hotel began the tradition of hosting United States Presidents, beginning with Benjamin Harrison, who attended a lavish reception in his honor on the piazza—and watched with horror as part of the floor dropped eight feet.

The Antlers was at the height of its glory when on October 1, 1898, the hotel was destroyed by a fire. The blaze had started in the railroad depot a few blocks away and before it could be stopped had consumed the entire hotel. As soon as the extent of the disaster became known, a telegram was dispatched to General Palmer, who was traveling in England on business. The saddened General acted immediately and cabled back that he would build a new hotel on the site, twice as grand as the old one.

And he did. The second Antlers Hotel, Italian Renaissance style with Spanish and French and Swiss embellishments, was begun at once. Six architects had submitted designs for the enormous new Antlers, and the contract went to Varian & Sterner, the firm that had designed the Greenbriar Hotel in White Sulphur Springs as well as an impressive number of fine Denver buildings. Constructed of cream-colored brick with white stone trim and a red tile roof, the new Antlers had ten loggias, sixty Florentine balconies, and a green and white awning at each window. Five stories high on the Cascade Avenue side, seven on the depot side, the hotel cost $600,000.

Two flights of stone stairs led from the north and south to a common landing, a third flight to the grand entrance which opened into the imposing west lobby. Besides two hundred guest rooms, the Antlers had a variety of public rooms decorated with the most lavish European features—Roman mosaic floors, Flemish oak beams, French windows, Spanish leather chairs, and Gobelin draperies. In addition to the many public rooms, the Antlers had an East Indian sunroom and an enormous ivory and cerise ballroom with a white maple floor.

When the new Antlers opened on July 2, 1901, it was the pride of Colorado Springs residents as well as Eastern guests who were charmed with the hotel's frankly snobbish appeal. "The Antlers does not cater to cheap patronage and its prices are sufficiently high to insure the best quality of everything," an early brochure assured its clientele.

Theodore Roosevelt, who had delighted the members of "Little Lunnon" quite as much as he had the social circles of the East, had remarked once that Colorado was the "playground for the entire Republic," and the Antlers had been quick to apply his words to the hotel—that is, as long as the members of the Republic who played there were socially acceptable and could afford to pay their bills. For their pleasure, the Antlers advertised riding, driving, automobiling, golf, polo, tennis, cricket, croquet, lawn bowling, trapshooting, coaching, cross-country riding, coyote and jack rabbit hunting, and mountain climbing.

The Antlers, "always headquarters because it is conceded to be the best hotel in the West," also offered to its guests that special Colorado commodity, the road to health:

> If the facts could be impressed upon the inhabitants of our central and eastern states, that when they are confined to their farms and houses for weeks at a time by snow and slush and ice, and the sun is seen so seldom as almost to be forgotten, that they were within one day's ride of a country where snow and slush and ice never interfere with comfortable travel, and where the almost perpetual sunshine invites them to an outdoor life almost as strongly as in summer, me thinks there would be thousands . . . who would hasten to genial Colorado.

And, of course, to no one's surprise, particularly the Antlers', they did hasten. From Presidents who sought the limelight, such as T. R., to millionaires who didn't—Winfield Scott Stratton, the former carpenter who had discovered one of the richest gold mines on earth, the Cripple Creek Independence, and hid in the Antlers' men's room to escape the embarrassing proposals of love, legal and otherwise, from ambitious women.

One of the greatest Antlers' coups, that set the social seal of approval on the hotel's snob appeal, came in 1915 when etiquette arbiter Emily Post stayed at the hotel—and approved of it enthusiastically in her book *By Motor to the Golden Gate*. Her description of the typical guest at the "big splendidly kept hotel with its broad white hallways, wide verandas and sunny terraces" would have shocked less sophisticated travelers than those who stayed at the Antlers: "He plays all games recklessly; he drives a powerful motor-car, and he is flirting outrageously with one of the prettiest women imaginable, whose invalid husband seems to care very little how much attention she accepts from her ardent admirer."

Less officious than the young men but equally enamored with the Antlers was Katharine Lee Bates, author and song writer, who composed "America the Beautiful" in her Antlers room after returning from a trip to the top of Pikes Peak.

Benjamin Harrison had set a precedent when he visited the old Antlers in the 1890's, and the hotel became a favorite Colorado spot for most of his successors. Teddy Roosevelt came, of course, and gave one of his rousing speeches from the hotel balcony. The crowd stretched almost a block down Pikes Peak Avenue to watch as Teddy swept off his pince-nez and yelled, "Can everybody hear me?" William Howard Taft appeared at the Antlers early in his campaign to capture the Republican Presidential nomination. Senator Warren G. Harding made clear his desire to be President while staying at the Antlers. Even that "also ran" William Jennings Bryan stopped at the famed hotel.

If the early Antlers' guests were colorful, so was the staff—

The first Antlers Hotel, Colorado Springs.

headed by manager Henri Marucchi, a commanding Frenchman who wore English plaid suits and sported a vast mustache. William S. Dunning, his capable assistant, paid court to the young ladies, while maître d'hôtel M. Berget, straight from Paris, charmed their mothers. Much admired for his reverent air when seating favored guests for a nine-course dinner, M. Berget was an indispensable guide for social acceptance. When M. Berget personally delivered hot cross buns to a Springs resident on Good Friday, that person had arrived socially.

One of the few Colorado Springs residents who didn't need M. Berget's special attentions to point out her enviable social position was Mrs. Joel A. Hayes, the daughter of Jefferson Davis and a close friend of General Palmer's despite the fact that the General and his cavalry unit had nearly captured her father. The friendship almost ended, however, in 1907 when the General, hosting a reunion of his old regiment at the Antlers, decorated the lobby with a poster offering a $360,000 reward for the capture of the Con-

The west terrace of the old Antlers, where Mrs. Forrester sipped old-fashioneds at sunset. (*Denver Public Library Western Collection*).

federate president. With great bitterness, Mrs. Hayes denounced the General and demanded that the poster be removed, and General Palmer, not only a friend but a gallant of the grandest sort, finally ordered the offending decoration taken down.

The Antlers caused the beginning of its own decline as far back as 1910 when the management criticized the parties given by some of its guests, at least one of whom promised that he would build a a hotel to put the Antlers in the shade—and the result supposedly was the Broadmoor, opened in 1918 with Billy Dunning, the Antlers' pet, as its manager. But though the Broadmoor tarnished some of the Antler's shine, the old hotel managed to hold its own until World War II. Extensive restorations (one costing more than the original construction) and various remodelings failed to appeal to later generations. So the fine old Antlers, "always headquarters because it is conceded to be the best hotel in the West," was torn down in 1964 to make room for a multimillion-dollar office complex.

At the height of its popularity, in 1898, the Antlers (*above*) burned in a fire that consumed the Colorado Springs railroad depot as well. The second Antlers, more popular than the first, was built in Italian Renaissance style (*Denver Public Library Western Collection*).

A horde of Presidents, celebrities, and social nabobs visited the Antlers before it was torn down in 1964 (*Denver Public Library Western Collection*).

28. The Only Hotel of That Name in All the World (*Boulderado*)

"Last night the principals of the Amelia Bingham company went to Denver in automobiles because Boulder lacked any hotel facilities," wrote an indignant *Daily Camera* reporter citing the disgraceful lack of a first-class hotel in Boulder. Local business leaders were all too painfully aware of the city's deficiency and had tried for a long time to interest backers in financing a hotel. When attempts made over a number of years proved unsuccessful and the list of potential financiers was exhausted, the city fathers decided that the only way to obtain a first-class hotel in Boulder was to build it themselves.

Accordingly, in early 1906, they formed the Boulder Com-

133

mercial Association, later the Chamber of Commerce, to issue and sell $100,000 worth of stock in a Boulder hotel. Each of the eighty men present at that initial January meeting "pledged himself to go out with his committee and talk hotel. Rattling speeches were made by several citizens." Despite those enthusiastic talks and speeches, described as "at once witty, happy and able," subscribers had pledged only $60,000 at the end of six months, just slightly more than half of the amount necessary to build and furnish the proposed hotel.

In an effort to push stock sales, the *Daily Camera* published an architectural drawing of the $80,000 proposed structure and a stripped-down version of the hotel that the $60,000 would buy. The larger building was to be built of red brick with buff trim and would have seventy-six sleeping rooms, ten suites. Sample rooms would be on the fourth floor, servants' quarters on the fifth. The roof would have private dining rooms "a la roof garden," one in each of its four corner towers. The main dining room was to be decorated with fluted Corinthian columns, paneled walls and ceilings, and heavy wainscoting, all in stained cherry wood with a rich mahogany effect.

The $60,000 smaller version of the hotel would be only four stories and constructed all of red brick with no trim. It was to have the same number of sleeping rooms but only six suites. Sample rooms would be on the third floor, and servants' quarters and roof garden were forgotten. The dining room would be finished merely in pine.

The newspaper stories and sketches apparently spurred stock sales since before the year was out $94,100 worth of stock had been sold, and the architect was drawing final plans. Soon construction bids were taken, and R. P. Basta, whose bid of $55,000 was $14,000 lower than the next estimate, was given the job of building the hotel. The hotel's financial problems weren't over yet, for competing contractors claimed that Basta couldn't possibly do an adequate job on his low bid price and claimed that at that cost his work would be inferior. "The great Boulder hotel, Boulder's pride, awaits while the contractor dilly dallies," reported the *Camera*. "It is clearly up to the directors to cut the Gordian knot."

Eventually the contractor dilemma was solved, and the Commercial Assocation moved on to its next problem, that of selecting a name for their hotel. The newspaper liked the idea of naming the building after a local civic leader and suggested two men, A. J. Macky and William R. Rathvon, the latter the head of the Commercial Association. Macky, whose name had been presented while hotel funds were uncertain, declared, "I do not wish my name to be used on a thing that it not in existence," while Rathvon declined with the warning that it wasn't smart to name something after a man still living. Rathvon suggested the name "Boulderado," a composite of "Boulder" and "Colorado," and immediately entered into a hassle with the *Daily Camera* over his choice. He wrote to the newspaper defending the name:

> In casting about for a suitable name for the hotel, we realized that we wanted something original, unique and euphonious. The West is full of "Grands" and "Palaces" and Grand Views" and the like, which mean little or nothing to the traveler who drops his grip on the floor as he registers. Hence when the name "Boulderado" was suggested . . . it was significant and distinctive. . . . It will be the only hotel of that name in all the world.

The *Camera* retaliated with a story entitled "Oh What's In A Name?":

> Two gentlemen were overheard by a bright Boulder lady on the train yesterday:
> "They've got a new hotel in Boulder," said one.
> "Yes, what do they call it?"
> "They call it the Boulder-a-do," and he gave a broad accent on the a.
> And all the while we were flattering ourselves that there was a pretty addo sound to it that might reconcile us to the offenses against the proprieties of language and rhetoric. Why not Hasherado?

After exchanging a number of wordy barbs in the *Camera's* columns, Rathvon finally hired a stonemason to chisel "Boulderado" above the entrance to the hotel, and that settled the argument.

After nearly ten years of planning and soliciting, Boulder's first-class hotel at last opened, on December 31, 1908. Final cost of the furnished hotel was $138,000, more than its builders had intended, but the structure and its *décor* were everything the city fathers had hoped.

"Boulder's Magnificent Hotel Is Thronged With Surging Crowds of Admiring Visitors," proclaimed the newspaper following the hotel opening:

> Last night's visitors at the Boulderado were charmed with the beauty of the furnishings, the size and airiness of the rooms, the arrangements of the suites and the magnificence of the effect of its entirety. The spacious dining room with its snowy linen, polished silver and delicate bouquets that are to come . . . The handsome electric chandeliers, the exquisitely patterned rugs, the profuse decorations of palms, ferns and flowers, the beautiful music of the orchestra, all added to the sum to make a perfect total.

Boulder was destined to become one of the first, if not the first, of pre-eminently residential cities in the Rocky Mountain region, prophesied the reporter. "For it has the necessity requisites . . . and a fine hotel like the Boulderado."

The hotel was indeed an asset to Boulder. It stood five stories high of brick and native stone with a wide gallery on each floor. Through entrance doors of beveled and leaded glass, hotel guests walked across a mosaic tile floor to a desk set in a wall paneled in cherry wood. Two floors above was suspended a false ceiling of cathedral glass imported from Europe. The hotel had a hollow center, and a skylight on the top floor directed sunlight through the multicolored roof to the lobby. Cantilevered over fully a fourth of the lobby was the massive paneled stairway, which rose in indented tiers to the top floor. The first-floor landing was large enough to hold an entire band, and for years fraternity and sorority dancers promenaded in the lobby to a band playing just a few feet above their heads. The hotel in its early days provided the setting for many weddings in which brides in their long white gowns descended the handsome stairway to the ceremony in the lobby. In the past few years, the Boulderado has been host to several couples married in the hotel, who have returned to celebrate their fiftieth anniversaries.

Just off the lobby was the paneled dining room with a patterned tile floor and half-circle stained-glass windows matching the cathedral ceiling in the lobby. Near the dining room was a men's smoking room, since guests, of course, were not allowed to smoke at the Boulderado's dinner tables. A card room and various offices and shops were on the first floor.

Opened as a commercial hotel catering to railroad travelers, the Boulderado also hosted many University of Colorado visitors. Entertainers performing at university functions along with conference guests, such as Robert Frost, always chose the Boulderado as a stopping place. Matrons whose daughters planned to attend the university sometimes rented suites a year in advance so they could escort their girls to college and provide support during sorority rush weeks.

Designed as an elegant but nevertheless practical hotel that would appeal to everyday travelers and businessmen as well as wealthy vacationers, the Boulderado remained a successful hotel by fitting itself to the eras it served.

No more do the principals of the Amelia Bingham or any other company have to go to Denver because Boulder lacks hotel facilities. Today they can select from a dozen Boulder hotels and motels. They can choose modern or gaudy, cozy or quaint, but if they want real elegance, they still check in at the Boulderado.

"Hotel that we aspire to have" (*left*). "Hotel we have present money for."

The citizens rallied and built the better of the two (*above*). Below a suspended ceiling of cathedral glass an elegant stairway was cantilevered over fully a fourth of the lobby.

29. The Finest Hotel in the World
(Brown Palace)

At the time the Brown Palace opened its onyx halls to the traveling public, a reporter for the *Chicago Century* wrote, "The three finest hotels in the country are in Denver, San Francisco, and Chicago. The Palace Hotel of San Francisco, the Auditorium of Chicago and the H. C. Brown Palace of Denver are unsurpassed by any others in the world; between these three and all the rest so great a gulf has been fixed that comparison is useless."

Miffed by the Chicago reporter's account, a *Denver Republican* writer declared unabashedly, "The *Century* writer did not quite state the situation by placing the San Francisco Palace and the Chicago Auditorium on exactly the same level as the H. C. Brown Palace of Denver. The latter is unquestionably the finest hotel in the world."

Nine floors of handsome Italian Renaissance architecture, built of Arizona sandstone and filled with Louis XIV and XVI antiques, 440 rooms and worth something over $1,000,000, the H. C. Brown Palace of Denver—if writers quibbled literally about its national standing—was, anyway, among the finest hotels ever built.

It was erected on a triangular cow pasture at the foot of Brown's Bluff, only recently renamed "Capitol Hill," the site of Denver's most lavish homes. The strangely shaped plot of land on Broadway had had little appeal to merchants, and its owner, unable to sell at his price, finally decided to build a hotel on the site, after interesting William Bush and Maxy Tabor in supplying part of the costs. It was Bush who named the hotel the H. C. Brown Palace.

The immense lobby of the Brown—the name by which the hotel soon became known to habitués—rose tier upon tier eight stories to a stained-glass interior roof. The lobby floor had an immense fireplace on the Seventeenth Street side (it is still there but it has a glass display case where the opening and flue used to be), a decorative fountain in the center, and onyx walls all round. (The Brown Palace had used 12,400 feet of onyx in the decoration, more than had ever been commissioned for a building before, an obvious inspiration to reporters, who frequently commented on the luxury. The Brown Palace itself hired a promotion man who extolled the virtues of the stone: "One fancies the gnomes who for centuries so jealously guarded the mine, stealing from countless beds of tropical flowers their choicest tints and embalming them in exquisite stone.")

The best view of the lobby, maintained one admirer, was from the eighth-floor balcony where one could look down on the tile floors bordered with Greek fret designs and watch the "electric lights shining upon the polished onyx wainscoting and illuminating the stained-glass roof overhead, the moving crowds, the bustle of arrival and departure."

Instead of clustering its public rooms on the first floor, the Brown Palace arranged them throughout the hotel. Decorated in Louis XVI style with delicate shades of cream and gold, the grand salon, on the second floor, was furnished with white mahogany pieces, softly shaded silk hangings, ivory-toned columns garlanded with gold, and "overhead an immense central medallion in the Watteau tints . . . blue clouds and soft fleecy clouds amid which rosy, blossom-wreathed cupids disport themselves."

The dining room several stories above, on the eighth floor, was another "sybaritic paradise for the aesthetic eye." Two stories high with an onyx wainscoting that reached five feet, the main dining room was decorated in olive green with columns of stucco work "perfectly representing massive carvings of Japanese ivory." Smaller dining rooms—a ladies' ordinary finished in old pink, a club room in terra cotta, three private rooms in light blue and three in olive—and a massive banquet hall surrounded the main dining room, and all were fitted with specially designed china, silver, and linen.

The Brown Palace was designed with five bridal chambers "too beautiful and delicate for use." Declared the hotel promotion man in his flowery pamphlet, "Hopeless old maids and bachelors would be legally justified in hanging themselves or each other, after a view of these lovely apartments . . . in tints which might have been copied from a maiden's blush." The rooms were decorated with a continuous tracery of lacework and delicate flowers, marguerites and forget-me-nots. The carpets used the same floral designs. In one room "the feet seem to sink in a field of daisies"; in another "the path of the bride is literally strewn with roses." For a day's bliss in one of the bridal bowers, a groom could pay as high as $100. Newlyweds were the favorites of hotel employees, declared a reporter who wrote, "The hotel people vastly prefer the brand newly married as guests. Everybody else is at times morose and sour."

The rest of the bedrooms, half with private baths, many with fireplaces, were decorated in fifty shades of yellow—cream to gold. "It would require a genius for nomenclature to catalogue all the charming effects that have been produced from a lump of ochre, and it would take a Raphael a lifetime to reproduce them."

Under the management of N. Maxcy Tabor and the ubiquitous William H. Bush, the Brown Palace opened in August, 1892, in time to host the twenty-fifth Triennial Conclave of the Knights Templar. Thousands of knights swarmed through the onyx walkways of the Brown, which had been handsomely festooned in their honor. But no room had been decorated as handsomely as the banquet hall, its immense horseshoe-shaped table set with baskets "piled high with luscious fruits sun-kissed and glowing, from the Pacific slope." The lavish banquet was "christened with rich vintages mellowing for years in the cellars of aristocratic millionaires brought hither in honor of that memorable week." The Brown overlooked no small detail in preparing the grand banquet, but unfortunately its sleeping rooms hadn't been finished in time for the convention, and the "brother sir-knights" were unceremoniously piled on cots in some of the larger rooms.

From the moment it opened, the Brown Palace was considered by many to be not only the finest hotel in the world but also the most fashionable. Frank Ellinger, the "terribly fast young man" in Willa Cather's *A Lost Lady,* lived at the Brown Palace, and Neil, the young hero, "liked to sit in the diningroom of the Brown and watch the elegant women as they came down to dinner—fashionable women from 'the East' on their way to California." (Inconsequentially, Miss Cather's story was set in the 1880's and the Brown Palace wasn't built until the 1890's, but the anachronism just pointed out the timelessness of the Brown.)

Of course, there were real people who stayed at the hotel, and they ranged from Presidents to celebrated entertainers. Lillian Russell preferred the bridal suite during her visits. Mary Garden was a quiet, pleasant guest though not nearly so solemn as William Jennings Bryan. Harry Lauder delighted the staff with his merry parties filled with laughter and song. Florenz Ziegfeld and wife Anna Held were indignant guests who attempted to check into the Brown Palace with her dog Blackie. Told by the desk clerk that the hotel never allowed animals, the couple threatened to have the young man fired, but the employee held his ground, and the disgruntled pair had to stay in their private railroad car. Evalyn Walsh McLean brought a different kind of pet whenever she stayed at the Brown—her Hope diamond.

An early hotel guest was German Count Koenigsmarcke, who had left Brandenburg after pulling a boyish prank. The Count traveled the country in high style and stayed in Denver, of course, at the Brown Palace. When his money ran out, the Count promptly became the hotel's bookkeeper and continued to charm staff and guests for more than a year, when he was allowed to return home.

As the most fashionable hotel in Colorado, the Brown Palace was the scene of Denver's most celebrated *cause célèbre,* centered in a quarrel between two men—balloonist Tony Von Phul and gentleman-adventurer and mine promoter Frank Harold Henwood.

The two men met one night when they were staying in the Brown Palace. For several days after that, they engaged in a series of verbal bouts and at least one fist fight. Then one night as they both were drinking in the Brown Palace bar, Von Phul put his finger into Henwood's wine glass, calling him a foul name, and the enraged Henwood pulled a gun and shot his companion. After the assault Henwood calmly walked to the lobby and waited docilely for the police while Von Phul lay on the barroom floor declaring that the two had disagreed about the relative merits of the beauties in the current Follies. Von Phul refused an ambulance and insisted on riding to the hospital in a taxi, and died shortly afterward. Not one to be outdone by his victim, Henwood claimed that the argument began when Von Phul, a wine connoisseur, did once too often what he frequently did to the annoyance of his friends, namely dip his finger in Henwood's wine to taste it, whereat Henwood objected, and the two started quarreling.

In a scandalous trial that shocked Denver for weeks, Henwood was found guilty of second-degree murder, not for the death of Von Phul but for killing a bystander. When the charge of murdering Von Phul was dismissed several months later, Henwood appealed the second-degree-murder verdict. Expecting a quick acquittal, the astonished Henwood was declared guilty of first-degree murder at the second trial and sentenced to life imprisonment. He died in jail in 1929.

More important skirmishes than the Henwood–Von Phul fight took place in the Brown Palace when visiting Presidents and would-be chief executives stopped at the hotel to plan campaign strategy. From the time of Theodore Roosevelt, politicians chose the Brown Palace as a stopping place, but the hotel's political aura reached a climactic brightness when Dwight D. Eisenhower named the Brown as his Presidential campaign headquarters in 1952. On frequent Colorado trips during his eight years in the White House, President Eisenhower always stayed at the Brown, soon dubbed the "Summer White House."

Through the years the Brown Palace changed its elegant *décor*. Leather-covered chairs in the lobby were replaced with bilious overstuffed sofas and later with another kind of leather couch. Bars and dining rooms were intermittently opened and closed and moved from here to there. During the 1930's the Ships Tavern, Colorado's most famous restaurant, was added, along with the murals which visitors now regard with amusement, of the old and then-new in transportation—a Wells, Fargo Concord stagecoach and a Ford trimotor airplane.

In 1959 the Brown Palace added across the street, a twenty-two-story annex, connected with the main building by a second-story, over-the-street walkway. Built and furnished for $4,200,000, more than twice the cost of the original hotel, the Brown Palace West was designed as a modern version of the older hotel. Instead of sandstone, the Brown Palace West was built of similar-colored mosite with exterior aluminum panels. Marble was put into the lobby in place of onyx. Sleek and comfortable as the new Brown Palace West is, however, most guests still prefer the rooms of the old Brown, as fashionable today as in 1892 when the hotel was acclaimed "the finest hotel in the world."

W. H. Jackson was an undauntable photographer of nearly completed hotels. (*Library, State Historical Society of Colorado*). The Brown Palace West, completed in 1959.

A good portion of the 12,400 feet of onyx commissioned for the Brown Palace was used in the lobby. "Christened with rich vintages mellowing for years in the cellars of aristocratic millionaires," the grand banquet room opened to host the twenty-fifth Triennial Conclave of the Knights Templar. (*Denver Public Library Western Collection*).

Decorated in Louis XVI style, the grand salon boasted "overhead an immense central medallion in the Watteau tints . . . blue clouds and soft fleecy clouds amid which rosy, blossom-wreathed cupids disport themselves." The luxury of the Brown Palace reached even into its many-fauceted bathrooms (*Denver Public Library Western Collection*).

Potted palms and bloated overstuffed furniture, latest *décor* of the 1920's.
(*Denver Public Library Western Collection*).

PART III

SPAS AND WATERING SPOTS

30. Buy a Ticket and Take a Plunge
(Royal Gorge)

Like toadstools after a rain, hot springs resorts pushed up all over Colorado to handle the mushrooming crowds of vacationers who liked to bathe in the pools, picnic in near-by woods, and promenade at Saturday-evening hops. A few of the resorts were highly successful and still attract tourists, but most led an up-and-down existence and finally, forgotten and forlorn, were razed or burned down by themselves.

Such a mildly successful resort was the Royal Gorge Hotel and Hot Springs, an ambitious name for a hotel whose glory lasted even less than a decade.

Dr. J. L. Prentiss, early-day physician and Canon City civic leader, analyzed the warm mineral waters at Royal Gorge Hot Springs and became enamored with the idea of building a great Western health resort rivaling the popular Virginia spas. In 1873, Dr. Prentiss acquired the property and erected a bathhouse. Then, encouraged by the success of his operation and the arrival of the railroad, he began construction on the Royal Gorge Hotel.

The thirty-eight-room building was erected on the banks of the Arkansas River. Two stories high with a number of dormer windows opening on a view that led to the Royal Gorge, the hotel was constructed of frame at a cost of $38,000. The finest room in the establishment, and one particularly popular with the local people, was the ballroom, which measured fifty by thirty feet. Near the hotel stood the bathhouse, built over a spring. There also was a tiny outdoor pool, no bigger than a bathtub, for those who liked to bathe outdoors.

"The bathing department has been newly fitted and heated by steam. The bath tubs are porcelain lined, and no pains have been spared to add to the comfort of our patrons," declared Dr. Prentiss in an early-day report. He added that his 101° waters were a "sure cure for rheumatism, skin diseases, kidney and liver complaints and general purifier of the blood."

During the mid–1890's the Royal Gorge Hotel and Hot Springs enjoyed its small streak of prosperity, though it is doubtful that the hotel cleared much of profit even then. Miners from Leadville, Rosita, Cripple Creek, and Victor were particularly fond of the springs, and the D&RG made a special stop in front of the hotel to let them off the train. A swinging footbridge across the Arkansas connected the hotel with the train stop.

Canon City residents were constant guests at the Hot Springs hotel for balls and picnics as well as for bathing. The *Canon City Weekly Record* noted editorially that it was good business to "buy a season ticket and take a plunge occasionally. Nobody has done more for the town than Dr. Prentiss."

Around the turn of the century when mining declined in Lake and Custer counties, business fell off at the Royal Gorge Hotel and Hot Springs. Fancier resorts in Colorado Springs drew away more vacationers, and in 1916 business ceased altogether when a flood in near-by Phantom Canyon destroyed the D&RG tracks.

In 1925 the property was sold for $40,000 to a man who attempted unsuccessfully to rejuvenate the hotel and hot springs. Twenty years later he sold the place for a quarter of his purchase price to an Oklahoma group which planned to offer it to the Church of God for use as an orphanage. The state, however, would not approve the building because it was located too close to the river. The Royal Gorge Hotel, for all its ambition, was boarded up once again and a few years later joined most of its ilk as a victim of the wrecker's ball.

The Royal Gorge Hotel differed from other hot springs resorts of its class only in name (*Library, State Historical Society of Colorado*).

31. Sound in Every Particular
(Trimble Springs)

Three buildings claimed the name "Trimble Hot Springs Hotel." Thomas F. Burns, a wealthy New Mexican, built the first one in 1882. T. D. Burns, possibly his son, built the second twenty years later or thereabouts. Nobody remembers who erected the third or even when it was built. They all burned down.

The springs were named after W. F. Trimble, appropriately their discoverer, who stumbled onto them in 1874. "Sorely afflicted with rheumatism," poor Trimble had been twisted out of shape for fifteen years, the result of wounds received in an Indian war. Less than a month at the hot springs, however, and Trimble was a cured man, "sound in every particular."

Such a natural wonder could not go unexploited very long, and under the direction of Thomas F. Burns, it didn't. Trimble had attempted to run a way station and boardinghouse at the site of the springs, nine miles from Durango on the D&RG line, where he kept a bathhouse plastered with testimonials of remarkable cures which the hot springs had affected on those whom medical science had given up as hopeless. (Trimble averred that the waters effectively cured the tobacco habit, too.)

Evidently Burns was much taken with Trimble's claims, and after witnessing what he considered to be an absolutely miraculous cure, he decided that Trimble Hot Springs was ripe for picking. So Burns built the first Trimble Hot Springs hotel—a two-story frame building with a long veranda and a cupola—and added a bathhouse and a pavilion and a lawn as lavish as the claims he made for the waters.

Built at a cost of $25,000, the hotel had a kitchen, dining room, office, and billiard hall on the first floor, a parlor and fourteen guest rooms on the second. "The exterior design is very handsome and the interior is elegantly finished and admirably arranged for comfort and convenience," declared the *Denver Tribune*.

As the scene of the miracles to take place during Burns's regime

153

at the hot springs, the bathhouse, copied after one at Las Vegas, New Mexico, was "equipped in the most approved modern style with almost every kind of bath known." Like the others in Colorado, the Trimble Hot Springs bathhouse was declared to be "the most complete of its kind in the United States."

Burns lost no time in heralding the glad tidings to the afflicted, who flocked to the springs in masses seeking the miraculous cures. Possibly Burns's greatest source of income, however, was not the hopelessly ill but the helpless well—the Silverton miners who spent a few days a month there recuperating from payday sprees.

Neither the drunks nor the cripples apparently affected the holiday spirit of the hotel's third group of guests, the pleasure seekers from Durango who chartered special trains to take themselves to Trimble for picnics. "Trimble Springs is not only a health resort, but the place appears to be headquarters for events of a convival nature in La Plata county," reported the *Rico News*.

The hotel obviously was successful, for when it burned down in the mid–1890's, T. D. Burns immediately erected another to take its place, this one a fireproof three-story brick.

Built with another veranda and cupola, the second Trimble Hot Springs Hotel had forty rooms "as bright and neat as good taste can dictate and labor accomplish." A bar, billiard hall, bowling alley, and gymnasium were in a second building, the pool in a third. The grounds were adorned with walks, driveways, lawns, groves, and gardens in which "nature and art have vied with each other in putting the finishing touches to a charming and picturesque landscape." At the end of the lawn was the D&RG depot.

Though Trimble Hot Springs continued to think of itself as a place of unparalleled cures, the cripples began hobbling away to other spots, leaving their places to an influx of Silverton miners who decided that getting drunk in one town and sobering up in another was a waste of time and that they might as well do them both at the same place. The hotel also entertained fraternal orders and social clubs who liked the dancing pavilion and the family-style Sunday dinners. Although far from the miracle-water resort of

Trimble's time, his springs were highly popular until the second Hot Springs Hotel—the fireproof one—burned down, too.

The third hotel was made from a frame house which one of the Burnses had built at the edge of the hotel lawn. It was simply uprooted and hauled across the road to be converted into a boardinghouse. By the time the third building had been firmly implanted on the Trimble Hot Springs Hotel site, however, the type of business at the resort had changed, and so had the customers.

In the 1930's, two men reportedly on their way to the hot springs were arrested for carrying a gambling wheel in the back of their truck. As their defense they claimed that they were taking the wheel to a church bazaar. "If you believe these men were on their way to church, acquit them," the prosecuting attorney admonished the jury. Apparently the jury didn't believe they were and found the men guilty—and with them the reputation of the Trimble Hot Springs Hotel resort. Far from the serene haven of the sick of the 1880's the Trimble Hot Springs Hotel became just another road-house—pink stucco and glass block—until in 1963 it, too, burned down.

The best two of the Trimble Hot Springs hotels (*Library, State Historical Society of Colorado*).

The charred pink skeleton of the third hotel.

32. The Most Fashionable Watering Place
(Cliff House)

In an 1873 account, socially prominent writer Eliza Greatorix called Manitou Springs "the most fashionable and delightful watering place in Colorado." That was the year when the owners of the Cliff House, fussy, fancy hostelry to be known by the elite from coast to coast, began construction of their hotel.

When it opened in 1874, the Cliff House was far from the rambling, pretentious dwelling it would become. The hotel, known in early years simply as "The Inn," was a modest boardinghouse with twenty rooms. An early *Rocky Mountain News* article reported shortly before the hotel opened, "This house will be completed and opened to the public June 1st, 1874. It contains . . . large, finely lighted and well ventilated rooms." The account noted that the hotel was "located within a few yards of those wonderful mineral springs, Shoshone, Navaho, Manitou and Comanche." All fixtures, according to the *News*, were "new and complete," and the hotel boasted a billiard hall. The furnishings, however, were sparse, and a few of the beds were covered with tanned buffalo hides. There were better places to stay in Manitou, and business at The Inn was poor.

A couple of years after The Inn opened, Edward Erastus Nichols leased the unsuccessful hotel from its owner, a man named Keener. The new manager renamed the hotel the "Cliff House," opened the seasonal resort on a year-round basis, and enticed the triweekly stage from Colorado Springs to Leadville to use the building as its Manitou station. Business picked up considerably; in fact, the Cliff House was so successful under Nichols that guests frequently had to bed down in tents in the side yard since the rooms in the hotel were often filled.

> When we came here almost three weeks ago, it was intending to stay but as many days, but the days have lengthened into weeks and yet we defer our departure. Manitou deserves the name of the "Saratoga of the West." Our hotel—the Cliff—is most delightfully situated in the upper end of the narrow valley, within a stone's throw of the sulphur and two soda springs. . . . Mr. and Mrs. Nichols are very kind and obliging, and make their guests at home. The house is filled to overflowing, but there is always room for one more. There are a great many charming people here and much sociability, which makes the house very popular. But *the* event of the season in "Manitou" was the hop here last night.

The visitor writing in the *Rocky Mountain News,* August 3, 1879, expressed enthusiastically what most Cliff House guests felt about Manitou and their hotel. So successful was his operation that Nichols bought the Cliff House in 1880, adding wings to the main building and erecting a second structure near by. Eventually the two portions were joined to form the sprawling Z-shaped hotel that, stretched out, would have lengthened into a block-long structure. When the hotel remodeling was completed, Cliff House could boast of itself as one of the finest resorts in the country. Two shades of brown clapboard decorated with natural stone, it was a comfortable building with long verandas and porches filled with rocking chairs, which did not disguise the hotel's formal, fashionable air. The Cliff House was first class in every respect—from the cast-iron calla-lily fountain in the front yard to the flagpole atop the cupola.

The Cliff House lobby, an immense room stiff with Victorian furniture, was surrounded with archways decorated with carved fretwork—spindles, sunbursts, elaborate lacework. The exits led to a maze of hotel rooms—parlors, libraries, smoking and billiard rooms for men, ordinaries and sitting rooms for the ladies. All were decorated with a heavy Victorian hand—mahogany furniture upholstered in cut velvet, brass filigree light fixtures with blossom-shaped globes, brightly colored carpets laden with exotic flowers and leaves, filmy translucent curtains, occasional rocking chairs, and everywhere potted plants.

The dining room had a few delicate features. Big enough to seat four hundred, the room measured forty-eight by eighty feet. The cumbersome brick fireplace at one end was ponderous beside the pretty leaded-glass windows and carved sideboards, their drawers heavy with brass handles. Through a skylight the sun filtered down on window boxes filled with flowers and on gracefully molded bentwood chairs around white linen-covered tables.

On the upper floors were the bedrooms, many furnished with carved mahogany, pine, or maple pieces. Some of the rooms had iron or brass beds and pretty writing tables and marble-top dressers. Walls were covered indiscriminately with gilt-framed pictures— Gothic cathedrals, waterfalls, views of Pikes Peak, Roman games, athletic Gibsonesque maidens. The bridal suits, at the corner of the second floor, had a massive, ornate, highly polished brass bed, and an early *Rocky Mountain News* account noted without elaborating, "The bridal chamber is one of the novelties of the institution." The basement contained, as well as a tunnel to the baths and soda springs, a billiard parlor, barbershop, and several stores.

By the time Nichols had completed his rebuilding of the Cliff House, business was so good that he was competing successfully with some of Manitou's older, more established hotels. In fact, the old hotels suddenly found that they were the ones having to compete. When Nichols advertised the Cliff House as "immediately in front of the celebrated Manitou and Navaho Soda Springs," the Barker House noted, among other things, that it was "nearer the post office than any other hotel."

Business was so good, in fact, that Nichols soon found himself involved in a second major remodeling. When it was finished, the hotel had completed its present total of two hundred sleeping rooms, eighty-six private baths, two private dining rooms, and a large semi-detached ballroom which alone cost $15,000.

One of the first fine resorts in Colorado, the Cliff House found that it could offer its guests many of the entertainments of Eastern spas along with a purely Western atmosphere. The hotel organized camping trips, burro rides to the top of Pikes Peak (which took all day and most of the night as well), Indian dances on the hotel front porch. Those who wanted to relax could sit in rocking chairs on the veranda and sip tin cups of soda water dipped out of the spring a few yards in front of the hotel by little boys wearing rubber boots.

For the nearly seventy years that Nichols and his son, E. E. Nichols, Jr., ran the hotel, it was a popular, highly successful resort attracting visitors from all over the country. Thomas A. Edison, Lillian Russell, Theodore Roosevelt, even Aimee Semple Mc-Pherson were among those claimed as guests. Long after other resorts had fallen victim to decay and indifference, the Cliff House was a fashionable summer address.

Then, in 1945, E. E. Nichols, Jr., died, and the hotel was sold for the second time—then sold again and again. Its future looks as uncertain as its past was assured. Various owners have tried summer entertainments such as melodrama with only moderate success. Occasionally the hotel hosts conventions or club or college dinners, and the current owners have thought of turning the hotel into a retirement home. But for the most part things at Cliff House, after close to a century, are still.

The Cliff House shortly after it was graduated from "The Inn" (*Denver Public Library Western Collection. Photograph by Geo. E. Mellen*). The Cliff House advertised that it was "immediately in front of the celebrated Manitou and Navahoe Soda Springs."

The Victorian-encrusted ladies' parlor of the Cliff House. Backbone of
the Cliff House, the Gibsonesque matron (*Denver Public Library Western Collection*).

The Cliff House complex as it appeared about the turn of the century (*Denver Public Library Western Collection. Photograph by W. H. Walker*). The current Cliff House.

33. Equal to an Emergency *(Steamboat Cabin)*

It was typical of the puffed-up self-importance which small towns were attaching to themselves and their natural wonders that a nice little agricultural community at the end of the railroad would build a sand castle of wood just to host a convention. It was natural as well with the leftover frontier falderal, full of fancy and little reality, that the hotel wasn't ready in time for the convention, and visitors had to stay elsewhere. Even so, the townspeople credited the hotel with attracting to Steamboat Springs "a great deal of business and influence that should properly be ours." In a way, they were right, for what else but a fine resort hotel would entice wealthy Eastern visitors (albeit five or six families a season) to spend their summer in the northwest Colorado town?

Shortly before the railroad came to Steamboat Springs in early 1909, the town Commercial Club "emphasized the necessity of Steamboat Springs being in shape to properly care for the guests that will come here this summer," according to the *Steamboat Pilot,* and appointed seven of its members to devise means for building a fine hotel. Heading the committee was F. E. Milner, prominent banker and businessman.

The group suggested that to build the hotel the Steamboat Springs Town & Quarry Company would put up $15,000, the town $10,000, and five prominent citizens, including Milner, an additional $1,000 each. The club agreed to the plan and later upped the total figure to $50,000. The money was easily raised, and the *Pilot* reported, "We knew Steamboat Springs would rise equal to the emergency, and she has."

Like other businesses in town that liked to name themselves after parts of a riverboat, the hotel was to be called the "Steamboat Cabin."

Scheduled for a scant three- to four-month building period, the hotel missed its completion date by a wide margin and didn't open until fall, long after the grand opening set for midsummer.

But though it missed the important date, the hotel was well worth the delay to Steamboat residents. What was one convention compared with the thousands of guests who would flock to Steamboat later to stay in the fine Cabin Hotel? Three stories with an attic, the Cabin was U-shaped with a veranda running around three sides. Constructed of tan-colored shiplap siding outside and beaverboard inside, the Cabin was built to host a huge houseful, with one hundred sleeping rooms and a dining room that could accommodate, according to enthusiastic accounts, nearly six hundred. The hotel was designed, however, for a patient six hundred since the entire building contained only four bathrooms. The Cabin site was surrounded by pretty little springs, at least one covered with a fancy trocadero. The enthusiastic builders said that when the hotel was filled to capacity, the overflow could pitch tents around the springs.

Alas, for the builders; they never had to worry about tents in the backyard—or impatient lines at the bathroom doors, either. The Cabin never did have very many guests. At first it was successful enough. Said one Steamboat Springs resident, "Heck, the railroad ended there; you had to stay overnight." But along with the overnighters there were, fortunately, a few summer-long guests from the East who brought their families to Steamboat to spend the season sight-seeing or bathing at the Steamboat bathhouse.

Though not connected physically or financially with the hotel, the bathhouse, built at a cost of $30,000, had been opened shortly before the Cabin. "No Roman, even in the days of the opulent splendor of the Caesar's, ever enjoyed a luxury equal to this," declared an early Steamboat Springs brochure. And certainly the bathhouse was better than average anyway, with its 10 private pools, 5 showers, 8 tub baths, rubbing slabs, cooling rooms, parlors, barbershop, and 140 dressing rooms. It was a great attraction to Cabin guests who rode the hotel's tallyho back and forth to the pool to swim and relax.

Under a variety of owners and managers, the Steamboat Cabin Hotel was a tight ship for several years. But the business which city leaders believed would come to Steamboat with the railroad failed to show up, and after those first few years, the Cabin began losing money. Increasing motor travel brought frequent visitors to spend a night or two, but at the same time it mobilized the families who spent the summer at Steamboat, and gradually they stopped coming.

Finally, because of lack of business, the Cabin was closed and stayed locked for many years. Then, in 1937, Steamboat attracted the state cattlemen's convention only to discover that it had no place to quarter the stockmen, so a group of thirteen local businessmen arranged to underwrite hotel costs and open the Cabin for a few weeks. A couple was hired to manage the hotel, and after the convention, the two stayed on, renting rooms to local people and occasional guests.

Things began looking up for the Cabin. Although operating costs were high (during the winter months the hotel demanded close to ten tons of coal per month to heat the rooms), money started coming in. Prospective buyers began cocking their heads at the Cabin, and one went so far as to estimate costs for re-siding the building. Then one blustery cold winter day in January, 1939, the Cabin made the most (and possibly the only) newsworthy move of its career: it burned to the ground in less than an hour.

The Steamboat Cabin Hotel, Steamboat Springs.

The Cabin's lobby atmosphere (*above*)—armchairs and stuffed animals. The den was a popular gathering spot for summer guests. (*Denver Public Library Western Collection*).

During a January snowstorm the Cabin burned to the ground in less than an hour. Two guests, trapped in their rooms, were killed.

34. The Kissingen of America
(Hotel Colorado)

No hostelry in the entire Rocky Mountain area ever compared in downright snobbishness with "the Kissingen of America," the Hotel Colorado in Glenwood Springs. The aristocracy of America flocked to the hot springs resort at the edge of the Glenwood Canyon, and so numerous were the elite who visited the hotel that a special railroad siding had to be built to handle their private railroad cars—sometimes as many as sixteen at a time. (The front spot on the siding was reserved for P. D. Armour, packing-house magnate, except, of course, when a President of the United States was visiting Glenwood.)

Only proper Boston servants, who were not allowed to walk through the hotel corridors or grounds except when absolutely necessary, were hired to care for guests, and not only were Glenwood residents not employed by the hotel, they were forbidden inside the building.

Designed after the Villa Medicis in Rome, the Hotel Colorado was built around three sides of a large court. The central portion of the hotel had twin towers of red standstone fashioned after Italian belfries. A small open gallery ran across the façade of the fifth floor. The two lower stories were constructed of red sandstone, the upper three of cream-colored brick.

The lavishly terraced court was decorated with an eight-foot-deep pool in the shape of a parallelogram. In the center of the pool, which was well stocked with trout, was a fountain that shot a jet of water one hundred feet into the air.

Through an enormous porte-cochere, guests entered the rotunda, which ran nearly the length of the hotel. It was flanked with a ladies' ordinary, a private banquet room, a nurses' dining room, a children's playroom, and a ladies' billiard room with two tables (and a corner stand with an electrical teapot at which players could brew their own tea).

There were smoking and card rooms, a rattan parlor (set with wicker furniture), a gentleman's waiting room with fourteen roller-top escritoires, and various sitting rooms—the hotel called them "elegantly furnished drawing rooms, where the confidences of a tete-a-tete may be exchanged with every precaution of security and every safeguard of propriety."

The dining room, nearly 5,000 square feet, could accommodate several hundred guests—who were required to dress for dinner in formal attire. The walls were paneled with Texas pine wainscoting. The massive doors were grained and polished white poplar while the ceiling was pine "framed into little squares and constellated with electric globes," according to a newspaper account. At one end stood a great sandstone fireplace, and in the center of the room was an imported specimen of black-tailed deer "hugely antlered."

Its cuisine, claimed the hotel, was "not excelled in the country, and the choicest products of the fruitful valleys that lie around, together with exotics culled from China to Peru, furnish a menu that would satisfy the fastidiousness of Lullus." The *Philadelphia*

Inquirer described the hotel fare as "the fat of the land, cooked till it melts in your mouth."

The ballroom, which measured seventy-four by twenty-four feet, had pink walls above a light wood wainscoting. The floor was constructed of maple strips "as smooth as glass" and according to the hotel "would woo the most reluctant votary of Terpsichore." Fireplaces stood at either end, and five great windows looked out onto the valley.

Up the flights of stone stairs were two hundred bedrooms—a number of them in bridal suits—and nearly half that many bathrooms. Nearly all the guest rooms had open fireplaces, and most had brass bedsteads, some with testers gracefully wrought in arabesques. According to an article in the *Denver Republican,* "Each room has an extension electric globe whose height in front of a dressing table mirror a lady may regulate." Describing the *décor,* the account continued, "The upholsterer and the painter of the walls were furnished a sample of the carpet intended for each room, so that the tint of the walls and the effect of the furniture might be in harmony with each other and the tone of the Brussels upon the floor."

The corridors that bounded the vast rooms were described by an admirer as "a splendid conservatory in themselves," by the hotel as "long and stately corridors, where fashion's glittering parade can be seen to best advantage." The *Denver Times* wrote about the "tall Gibson type of beauty, with the arrogance of a princess, sauntering through the corridors."

An aboretum and a stone bridge over the road connected the hotel with the bathhouse, built in 1888. Constructed at a cost of $100,000, the bathhouse was built in Roman style with an elaborately landscaped lawn. The two-story building had forty-two rooms and a variety of baths.

A brilliant ball opened the Hotel Colorado on June 10, 1893, and many members of Colorado's English colonies attended the festivities that lasted several days. Special trains were scheduled from Denver, Colorado Springs, Pueblo, Leadville, and Aspen. Mr. and Mrs. Walter Devereux (part owners of the hotel) led the evening's grand march; according to a newspaper account, she was gowned in an "Elizabeth costume of lavender silk combined with brocade" and a glittering collection of diamond jewelry.

From the time of its grand opening the Hotel Colorado was held to be the poshest resort in Colorado, rivaling successfully the New York watering spots, attracting the wealthiest, most fashionable members of an elite society. "The summer girl was greatly in evidence at the hop at the Hotel Colorado Wednesday evening," wrote a *Denver Times* society reporter. "The strictly chaperoned debutante . . . is cautioned to participate in not more than perhaps two waltzes during the evening, but . . . would give her big blue eyes to, at that very moment be strolling through Lovers' Lane on the arm of some gallant." One newspaper noted that "reservations are rapidly coming in at the Hotel Colorado, and the rooms are nearly all engaged for the best part of the next three months," and followed the announcement with a column-long list of arrivals and another of social notes about the hotel.

While the strictly chaperoned debutante spent her days taking the baths—where she was required to wear long black stockings —or turning her big blue eyes on the black and white swans gliding around the ponds, her gallant was playing polo on the Glenwood Springs turf, riding one of the tough little $5 broncos that the cowboys trained and sold to players for $125. Or he was fishing at Trappers' Lake where "the fish are so abundant that they can be scooped up with the hands."

Not only the debutantes and their chaperones and young men spent their summers at the posh Hotel Colorado but some of the most colorful nabobs of the times visited the resort—Diamond Jim Brady, the Mayo brothers, Buffalo Bill Cody—and some of the most powerful. The hotel was so popular among Presidents of the United States that it was dubbed "the spring White House."

Theodore Roosevelt was Glenwood's most constant official guest, and he usually was accompanied by an entourage that included personal friends, photographers, naturalists, Secret Service men, newsmen, secretaries, and as many as five guides. During the spring of 1905, Roosevelt bagged ten bears and three lynxes during his Glenwood hunting trip. Displaying his skill on the Hotel Colorado lawn for photographers, he posed with one enormous bear to the amusement of his daughter, "Princess" Alice, who suggested that it be called "Teddy Bear," a name given to stuffed toys ever since. (Actually Clifford K. Berryman, cartoonist for the Washington *Star,* drew the first cub in 1902.)

That evening everyone who had participated in the hunt attended a stag dinner in the hotel's glittering formal banquet room, where they were sworn to secrecy about the stories told that night. Noticing the dismay of his guides at the array of silverware in front of them, Roosevelt told them, "Just grab the implement nearest you, boys!"

A few years later, in 1909, President William Howard Taft made a speech from the "Presidents' Balcony," the second-floor gallery facing the plaza, on which Roosevelt had given speeches. Taft arrived in Glenwood at 6:00 A.M. and stayed little more than an hour but found time to breakfast on wild raspberries and mountain trout. After visiting the Glenwood pool, he regretted that he didn't have time for a plunge and added, "But that's probably just as well. I've found it's much better for a fat man like myself not to bathe in public."

As elegant and as much sought after as the Hotel Colorado was, it couldn't weather the change in resort traffic—the demise of the summer-long visitor who was replaced by the stopover tourist. The hotel has been sold a number of times—for a while it was used as a wartime hospital—and in 1966 changed its name to the Village Inn, but its latter-day appeal never has approached its turn-of-the-century popularity. The silent Boston servants went home long ago, and a good number of years have passed since a private railroad car has been parked on the Glenwood Springs siding. Today the hotel that once forbade them to come through its doors is grateful for even Glenwood Springs residents.

The Hotel Colorado (*above*), Glenwood Springs, photographed by W. H. Jackson. The Palm Garden Annex to the dining room, a photograph made on a 1901 Polly Pry trip. (*Library, State Historical Society of Colorado*).

Elegant, if a bit rustic, the bathrooms (*left*) were a point of pride with the Hotel Colorado. While a young lady was flirting harmlessly with one of the eligible catchers at the hotel, her mother might be gossiping with other matrons in the parlor. (*Denver Public Library Western Collection. Photograph by W. H. Jackson*).

35. For Those Who Count on Expense
(*Stanley*)

When doctors gave Freeland O. Stanley only a few months to live, the plucky one-hundred-pound New Englander gathered together his wife, her maid, and his Stanley Steamer and headed for Estes Park, Colorado. The trio took the train to the end of its line in Lyons, and Stanley's wife and maid finished the twenty-mile trip by stage. The undauntable Stanley, however, was determined to drive his Stanley Steamer to the Park, regardless of the roads, declared impassable for automobiles. He puffed up his Steamer and rattled along the rocky roads of Big Thompson Canyon to reach Estes Park in a record one hour and fifty minutes.

F. O. Stanley was famous not only for the Stanley Steamer, which he had designed with his twin brother, but for other inventions as well. A child prodigy, he was an expert violinist and when only ten years old, invented a process for making the instrument. A few years later Stanley developed a new way of coating photographic plates and sold the process to George Eastman for $1,000,000. Along with his skill as an inventor, Stanley was an architectural designer, teacher, and student of political economy.

So it was not a commonplace invalid immigrant who steamed up the Big Thompson Canyon that day in 1902. F. O. Stanley was an extraordinary man, ready to contribute all his talents to the resort town of Estes Park. An energetic man despite his poor health, Stanley plunged into Estes Park affairs. Concerned that the Park didn't have a first-class hotel, he decided to build one, and with typical Stanley inventiveness, he designed it himself.

The hotel was patterned after New England resorts with which Stanley was familiar and copied after his Newton, Massachusetts, home. The architect Stanley chose a classic New England clapboard structure, four stories high, a center gallery flanked by two wings. Across the first floor ran a loggia where guests could sit in bentwood rockers and gaze across the Park floor to Longs Peak. A veranda for those who wished to sun themselves encircled the second floor.

Stanley, who picked the site because of its magnificent view, contrived to bring the spectacular mountain scenery inside the hotel. The dining room, at the southwest corner of the first floor, had spacious windows that took in the sweep of the Park.

The large, light lobby, laced everywhere with feathery arches, pillars, and delicate carving, was both charming and formal with a grand staircase that swept to a velvet-benched landing. On the floors above were the guest rooms, eighty-eight of them, filled with the best Grand Rapids furniture.

The double-duty music room kept the Stanley feeling of space and light with wide windows that opened onto a view of Estes. During the mornings the room was a writing area, a gossiping lounge, a sort of ladies' parlor, and was fitted with delicate writing desks and pretty chairs. During the afternoons the area became the music room with chairs grouped so that guests might listen to chamber-music concerts. Above the floor was a stage alcove with a carved grand piano where musicians under the direction of a concertmaster performed for the Stanley's patrons.

The billiard room was particularly fine since Stanley was an avid billiard player himself and prided himself on his skill. (A guest who snickered when Stanley missed a shot was asked to leave the hotel immediately.) In contrast to the lightness of the hotel, the billiard room was heavily paneled in dark wood and had massive raised benches cushioned with leather where ladies might sit to watch the games. Near the billiard room was the bar, similarly paneled and fitted with heavy pieces.

Not one to overlook any portion of his hotel, Stanley designed even the kitchen, one of the first all-electric kitchens in the country. Since Estes Park had no hydroelectric plant, Stanley built his own to supply the hotel and then furnished the rest of the town with his surplus power.

Along with the hotel, Stanley built the Stanley Manor, a smaller replica of the main building, a casino, stables, and his own home— all in the same New England clapboard style, painted a uniform resort yellow.

The Stanley—which was to have been called by another name until its builder acquiesced to local protests and named it after himself—opened on June 22, 1909, for a state convention of the Pharmacists' Association. The hotel's appeal was not local; it attempted to attract Easterners who could afford six weeks of elegant leisure in the Colorado mountains. Brochures and pamphlets issued soon after the hotel opened emphasized the Stanley's appeal to the wealthy class. The hotel advertised billiard rooms, bowling alleys, tennis and croquet courts, and a golf course:

> Golf on an ordinary course is exhilarating, but up here in the shadows of the great mountains, where the atmosphere contains the

elixir of life, the game is intoxicating . . . the old mountains echo the joyous shouts of the players as they amuse themselves on these grounds.

The hotel also was proud of its evening activities for guests. Besides dining, dancing to a "high class" orchestra, promenading around the grounds, and performing in amateur theatricals and concerts, the hotel offered guests a number of games to play:

> When the Orb of Day drops behind the mountain range and the shadows begin creeping toward the valleys, the atmosphere becomes gradually cooler, until after nightfall it is often quite chilly and one's system is properly attuned for an hour or so at the billiard table or the bowling alley.

In its brochure, the Stanley admitted quite candidly that "in the general plan of things earthly we must count on expense."

Fortunately for the Stanley, its guests did count on expense, and the hotel was run in a grand manner. Stanley himself was overlord, taking a personal interest in everything from operation of the kitchen's electric apppliances to maintenance of the fleet of Steamers that daily chauffeured guests up the Big Thompson Canyon to the hotel. Then in 1926, Stanley sold the hotel, the manor, the casino, and approximately 2,750 acres of land surrounding them, as well as the power plant, to the Stanley Corporation. Sale price was rumored to have been more than half a million dollars.

Though Stanley no longer was kingpin of the Stanley Hotel, he was still the "grand old man of Estes Park," credited with bringing modern tourist business to the town, and he still took an active interest in the hotel. During the 1930's, when the Stanley Hotel's business dropped considerably, it was rumored that Stanley himself sat in the hotel lobby watching guests who came to register. If he didn't like the looks of a visitor, he nodded unobtrusively to the desk clerk who told the traveler politely that the nearly vacant hotel was filled. In the early 1940's, Freeland O. Stanley, the man who came to Estes Park at fifty-four to live out his few remaining months, finally died at the age of ninety-three.

The grand old man was gone, but what about his grand old lady? Like many resorts, the Stanley Hotel was closed during the war years, and then sold shortly afterward. Unfortunately for the hotel, the generations of vacationers who believed that "in the general plan of things earthly we must count on expense" had died along with Stanley, and the hotel's problem was to find a new kind of guest. The solution went back to the day when the Stanley first opened its doors—with a convention. Now, though some of the Stanley guests are families or individuals, the bulk of the business during the Stanley's three-month season comes from conventions.

"In the general plan of things earthly we must count on expense"—the Stanley (*Library, State Historical Society of Colorado*).

177

The music room (*above*) and dining room shortly after the hotel was opened. (*Denver Public Library Western Collection*).

The Stanley complex today.

36. A Saratoga Free from Follies
(Radium Hot Springs)

If ever a Colorado resort had pretentions of rivaling the great
and glamorous Saratoga Springs in New York, it was the spa that
sprang up on the Soda Creek at Idaho Springs. The resort maintained that it had everything the folly-infested Saratoga had and
offered one advantage: the radium springs resort was sin-free.

"The purity of mountain air and the grandeur and beauty of
mountain scenery, inspire in all a love of the pure and good, and
will protect this beautiful retreat from the follies, vices, debauch-
eries and extravagances of fashionable watering places. This alone
should induce rich fathers and husbands to bring their fashion

and folly stricken daughters and wives to Idaho Springs—a Saratoga free from follies and crimes," claimed an 1871 Colorado travel director.

The springs on the Soda Creek had been discovered slightly more than a decade before the advertisement appeared, by a man named Jackson, who also was the first person to discover gold in the area. Coming over a rise in the mountains, Jackson saw smoke blowing from one of the canyons and feared it was from Arapaho campfires. When he crept nearer, however, he found that what he saw was not smoke from fires but vapor rising from a hot spring in the mountain, and not Indians but several thousand mountain sheep were camped beside the waters. Indians actually had journeyed to the hot springs before the white man came, to let their sick and wounded bathe in the healing waters. By common consent the area was neutral territory for warring Indian tribes, who shared the springs which they called "edah hoe," Arapaho for "gem of the mountains."

Shortly after Jackson's discovery, a prospector named James Jack and his son sank a mining shaft into the mountain near the spring. To their annoyance they had tapped an underground hot spring, and the hole kept filling with bubbling water. Disgusted, the pair gave up to prospect elsewhere and left the water-filled hole to occasional bathers.

A few years later, in 1863, Dr. E. S. Cummings purchased the property with the prospect hole, erected a cheap bathhouse, and charged the public for health bathing. Business was poor, so he sold the land three years later to Harrison Montague, who ran the hot springs for many years. Montague tore down the log shanty and built a stone bathhouse, called "Ocean Bath House," with separate sections for men and women and a swimming pool for both. By 1870 he had a popular business advertised as the "Saratoga of the Rocky Mountains." Denverites particularly were drawn to the springs and would drive up to take the baths and then dine at the exclusive Beebee House in Idaho Springs before returning to Denver.

While developing the baths, Montague also built a hotel to appeal not only to health seekers but to everyday travelers. Oblivious to danger, two characters who identified themselves as "Frank" and "Jesse James" signed the register, and a "William Bonney" (Billy the Kid) also signed it some years later. Sarah Bernhardt was a guest at the hotel, and so were Walt Whitman and H. A. W. Tabor.

Montague ran the prosperous though limited hot springs business until the turn of the century, when he sold it to a group of Idaho Springs businessmen called the "Big Five," for $60,000. The investors tried to raise money to build a first-class resort on their 160-acre property but found that the kind of establishment they wanted would cost far more than they could raise, so in 1910 they issued a ninety-nine-year lease to a stock company to develop the springs and spend $300,000 for buildings, equipment, and bathing facilities.

While selecting plans for the hotel, trocadero, swimming pool, tennis court, apartment building, and cabins that would cluster around the springs, the lessees decided to have the waters analyzed. Though healing qualities of the springs had been recognized since Indian times, it was not until the minerals were analyzed that the owners knew that the waters contained an amazingly high percentage of radium; in fact, the Idaho Springs water was the strongest natural radium water in the world.

The discovery caused a great deal of excitement among resort people, who predicted phenomenal business for the hot springs. John J. Hernan, manager of the fashionable Hotel Del Coronado at Coronado Beach, California, wrote, "If these radium waters of Idaho Springs were located in southern California, beyond question of doubt, they would form the nucleus for one of the big resort propositions of the country."

"I do not hesitate in saying that I consider it has one if not the most promising feature of any such resort I know . . . unlimited success," wrote Henry J. Bohn, editor of *Hotel World* and the leading resort authority in America. A *Rocky Mountain News* article stated, "Every year 150,000 people go to Hot Springs, Ark., 100,-000 travel to Mineral Wells and probably an equal number go to French Lick and West Baden and to the several hot springs of Virginia. . . . If this patronage comes to Colorado, it will contribute enormously to the prosperity."

Spurred by enthusiastic predictions, the Radium Hot Springs investors built a fine hotel to accommodate the thousands who would desert Eastern resorts for Idaho Springs. After discarding several designs, the lessees decided on a three-section building—a two-story center portion flanked by three-story wings. The center section actually was the old hotel which Montague had built, but to disguise it the architect covered the whole complex with white clapboard siding. A bridge over the Soda Creek connected the hotel with the road.

Radium Hot Springs, still bearing the mark of a Saratoga without sin, was concerned primarily with its baths, located in the basement of the hotel. An elevator took guests from the lobby to the horseshoe-shaped bath tunnel where they separated to go into the men's or women's baths. Each side could handle more than fifty bathers a day. The resort was equipped with a hot tunnel for men, one for women, cooling rooms, tub baths, massage areas, and a natatorium or swimming pool.

Since the early days of the resort, the healing powers of the springs had been recorded. "The hot soda springs of this place are gaining a world-wide reputation for their healing properties and people from both the old and the new world are annually flocking hither," wrote a newspaper reporter in 1881.

Once the springs had been analyzed, reports and testimonials flowed nearly as fast as the bubbling water. Claimed one account, "Cures almost miraculous have been so common in Idaho Springs that no longer do they excite any particular interest among the people of the village. It is an old saying in Idaho Springs that the stretcher is carried only in one direction." Another writer said that the people "leave their crutches and go away laughing, running and rejoicing."

Indeed, stories of the cures were commonplace, and for two fashionable decades health seekers did run and laugh in the atmosphere of the smart Radium Hot Springs. Until the late 1930's the springs were highly popular and attracted great crowds, among them guests bearing the names of Gould and Vanderbilt.

When World War II came, resort business at Idaho Springs slumped; and after the war, buying medicines from the corner drugstore became an easier way of curing illness than taking the baths at a resort hundreds of miles away. For several years business dropped considerably, then rose a little, and finally leveled off.

Just as folly-stricken ladies no longer promenade in the sinful Saratoga of the East, the guests in white linen no longer drape themselves in the white wicker chairs of the Saratoga of the Rocky Mountains. The era has gone and with it its fashionable leisure. Today the Saratoga of the West, Radium Hot Springs, is a bright, cheery hotel with a knotty pine atmosphere and only a wisp of the air that made it attempt to rival the great resorts of its time.

The first primitive bathhouse at Idaho Springs
(*Denver Public Library Western Collection*).

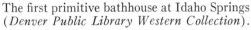

A lavish architectural sketch for the proposed Radium Hot Springs Hotel, later modified (*Denver Public Library Western Collection*). One of Colorado's few hot springs resorts to survive both the depression and World War II, Radium Hot Springs still does a respectable amount of business.

37. Monument to a Damned Fool
(Broadmoor)

The travel mania for watering spots was at its fashionable height in 1891 when Colorado Springs land promoter and dairyman Silesian Count James de Pourtales opened the first casino at Broadmoor. The eventual complex which Pourtales envisioned, clustered around his casino and an artificial lake, would include a hotel, cottages, and a series of connected walkways linking the various buildings.

Since Colorado Springs was not only a stuffy English colony and mecca for tubercular patients but an abstinent one as well, the Count, whose property was just outside the city limits, foresaw an excellent liquor business. He confided later, "The prices for the average run of spirits and cocktails are much lower in the East than in the West . . . and since Colorado Springs was a temperance city, I felt I could ask even higher prices."

As the Count suspected, despite those excessive charges, liquor flowed continuously in that formal, Georgian-styled casino. Even on Sundays one could get a drink at the Broadmoor since the Count countered clerical attacks for serving wine on the Sabbath with the notion that it was medicine for tuberculosis sufferers. (The clergy also attacked Pourtales' Sunday concerts, but the Broadmoor proprietor insisted that they were filled with sacred music—though he did slip in an occasional waltz when he thought he was safe.)

Liquor, the ambrosia of the Broadmoor casino, was also its poison. The Count at first was greatly pleased at the ready consumption of his wines and spirits, but after checking the liquor receipts, he discovered that most of his profits were strictly hypothetical.

Financial problems beset Count Pourtales early in his Broadmoor career; even before the casino opened he referred to the "present ugly financial situation." Expenses were high. The French cook whom Pourtales engaged declared that he could perform only on a so-called French cookstove, which had to be purchased and shipped from the East, and when it arrived, Pourtales found that the existing chimney in the casino kitchen was the wrong size and had to be torn out and rebuilt. Another expense was the constant replacement of silver spoons which kept disappearing. Pourtales discovered too late that the maître d'hôtel insisted on giving them as souvenirs to pretty ladies who visited the casino.

Transportation was another problem that plagued Count Pourtales from the beginning. He had counted on the streetcar line, which connected with most parts of Colorado Springs and ended at the casino's front door, to carry guests to and from the Broadmoor. Getting there was no problem, but the late-night trolly, which ran sporadically, could carry only a few of the hundreds of gamblers who trouped to the streetcar stop at casino closing time, and the rest had to wait in the cold for another car to ramble along. Added to that, the coaches consistently broke down.

In order to spur lagging business, which even on opening night wasn't up to expectations, the Count engaged in several promotional follies. He hired a lady balloonist to parachute onto the Broadmoor grounds, but she landed in the lake instead and nearly drowned. Then he engaged a tightrope artist to set off firecrackers from his highwire, but the performer nearly burned down the casino. Turning to safer pursuits, Pourtales decided to hold indoor parties for children, but the little ones wrecked nearly all the furniture.

Despite the fact that the Broadmoor was just about the only place in the area to buy a drink, only two years after the casino had opened, Count Pourtales admitted that he had failed, and the property was put into receivership. The Count went in search of another dream, an Arizona gold mine, and in this venture luck seemed to take a more favorable interest in him. The nobleman recouped his fortune in Arizona, and then retired to his ancestral estate Blumbowitz, in Silesia.

The Broadmoor casino burned down in 1897 and was rebuilt a year later, but the Count Pourtales never did redeem his property. The Broadmoor was held in receivership for many years until a notable sportsman, speculator, and millionaire, Spencer Penrose, purchased the property in 1916 and turned it into the eventual world-famous Broadmoor complex. Like the Count, Penrose never made a cent off the Broadmoor—he paid hundreds of thousands of dollars out of his own pocket just to keep the place open—but since, unlike Pourtales', the Penrose fortune didn't depend on a successful operation, he didn't much care. Penrose did remark once, though, that the Broadmoor was a "monument to a damned fool!"

The wealthy Penrose, who reportedly had purchased the entire Broadmoor 2,400-acre packet because he had admired a few lots of it, approached business associate Charles L. Tutt, and the two decided to build a fashionable hotel on the site of the second casino (which they uprooted and moved to a less conspicuous spot to be turned into the Broadmoor golf club).

Penrose hired the architect who had designed the Antlers Hotel in Colorado Springs as well as a number of lesser buildings throughout the state, Frederick J. Sterner, to incorporate his fustian ideas into a workable hotel plan. The outside, Penrose declared, was to be a pink terra cotta; the bedrooms would combine touches of Honolulu, Aix-les-Bains, and Lausanne; and the ballroom should give the illusion of the salon in the Peking royal palace. In addition, the architect should bear in mind that Penrose might someday move his entire Turkey Creek Ranch menagerie onto the grounds. The nightmarish combination was too much for Sterner, who resigned a nervous wreck to be replaced by more steely architects, Warren and Wetmore.

The new designers were better able to put up with Penrose's exacting ideas and threw a few of their own embellishments into the $3,000,000 structure, which emerged a nine-story Italian Renaissance affair with two wings, lavishly adorned and painted a fetching hue known as "Broadmoor Pink."

The hotel's rooms were handsomely decorated with hand-painted scenes on ceilings and walls, elaborate plaster work, and an immense curved marble staircase. There were a palm court in Pompeiian *décor* with lush vegetation and cozy nooks for afternoon tea; dining rooms in old ivory and Wedgewood blue tones and plaster latticework ceilings; a Georgian ballroom with marble pilasters, plum-colored hangings, and crystal chandeliers; an enclosed terrace facing the lake; and a lake plaza for dining alfresco. The bedrooms, each with a separate bath, some with private sleeping porches, were in French gray with cretonne hangings. Since Penrose and his wife were intrepid travelers, the rooms were decorated with rare Chinese antiques and valuable paintings.

The largest indoor pool in the West was supplied by mountain springs, or if one preferred other sports, there were squash courts, an eighteen-hole golf course, bridle paths, a polo field, tennis courts, and a lake for boating. In addition, the hotel boasted a fireproof garage, power and refrigeration plants, greenhouses, gardens, a dairy, beef and sheep pastures, and a piggery.

With a resort so lavish, Penrose felt it only fitting to invite John D. Rockefeller, Jr., as guest of honor at a select preview party attended by 1,000. Guests were entertained handsomely and served an exquisite supper, mostly French, with a dessert called "Comtesse de Cornet, Friandises," after Mrs. Penrose's daughter. About midnight Penrose realized that he hadn't greeted his guest of honor, who had arrived late in the afternoon just as the painters were adding last-minute touches, and was handed a note written by Rockefeller saying the smell of paint was so strong it gave him a headache, and he had moved over to the Antlers and gone to bed.

To no one's very great concern, particularly the owner's, the Broadmoor was a money-loser from the very beginning. Penrose was very generous, and if a friend fell into hard times, he could be sure of free room and board at the Broadmoor. Penrose liked to keep up a good front and during the depression years insisted on retaining a staff of one hundred even though at one time the hotel had only two guests.

Another expense was Penrose's flair for costly publicity despite the fact that it never brought very much in the way of returns. One of his stunts was to put up Jack Dempsey and his retinue in in the hotel while the pugilist was in training for the Gene Tunney fight. Dempsey obliged his host by posing for publicity pictures, putting on exhibitions in the ballroom wearing green silk tights, and generally going along with Penrose until the ordeal nearly wore him out, and he had to finish his training elsewhere.

Another reason for the Broadmoor financial quandary was that the hotel had opened during prohibition, and a good portion of any resort's profits, particularly one as posh as the Broadmoor, came from liquor. Penrose wasn't much concerned that prohibition affected his hotel's finances, but he was mad as hell that it kept him from buying a drink.

When the Broadmoor opened, Penrose had $250,000 worth of liquor stashed in a New York club (the fifteen-year storage charge on it was $28,000) and a reported $1,000,000 worth stored in a private, bonded warehouse. Rumor had it that he had hidden the larger supply in an abandoned Cripple Creek mine, which inspired another stampede to the mountains, a liquid gold rush that caused one old prospector to say that Penrose was the only man who ever salted a mine with whisky. To show his contempt for prohibition, Penrose shipped the emptied bottles from his New York cache to the Broadmoor for prominent display in the lobby.

Penrose's employees could be just as determined about their principles as their boss. One day the maître d' ventured into the tavern to settle a commotion and found a wealthy Texan calmly lunching while having his hair cut and his shoes shined. The maître d' told the millionaire firmly that the personal grooming would have to wait or the Texan could eat elsewhere. The guest insisted just as testily that he was going to finish luncheon and get his hair cut and his shoes shined all at the same time, and to back his stand offered the hotel employee a year's salary to let him do it. The maître d' staunchly, if sadly, shook his head, and the guest's attendants were escorted from the tavern.

Another firm restaurant employee, the dining room assistant maître d', turned away a guest whom he declared was not properly attired for dinner. Though wearing fine MacAfee riding boots, whipcord breeches, and an English tweed jacket, the gentleman, the employee insisted, was not correctly dressed for the hotel dining room. He had refused to admit, to his later dismay, Lucius Beebe, gourmet and perennial member of the country's list of ten best-dressed men.

Other hotel people could be just as firm as the dining room employees. One evening a Canadian playboy tried to lead his horse through the mezzanine to his room and found his way blocked by a determined lady who told him to take the animal right back to the stables.

"Who the hell are you?" he demanded.

"The housekeeper," she snapped. The next day the woman was introduced to the cowboy at a fancy hotel party—as Mrs. Spencer Penrose.

Though most major additions to the Broadmoor have been added since 1959—the Broadmoor South, the International Center, and the ski area, for instance—Penrose began the hotel's building program not long after it opened in 1918. In the early 1920's he donated his much-adored collection of Turkey Creek Ranch animals to the hotel, and kept them near the guests until a monkey bit a little girl, and her parents sued. Then Penrose decided to build the hotel's Cheyenne Mountain Zoo.

From a modest start with a few mountain animals and common zoo creatures, the Broadmoor began a collection of rare specimens, none of which ever attracted quite the attention meted out to that splendid elephant "The Empress of India, Gift of the Rajah of Nagapur to Spencer Penrose," who underneath the showy title was just "Tessie," a psychotic elephant whom Penrose had picked up from a circus friend at a bargain price.

Sometime later Penrose built the Broadmoor Riding Academy for indoor polo, later turned into the ice rink, and the Spencer Penrose Stadium, and his interest in construction even led him to build roads. He constructed one highway crisscrossing to the top of Pikes Peak, another stretching from the hotel past the zoo to the top of Cheyenne Mountain. He even paved the Broadmoor old stage road for automobiles, and to mark the opening of the newly asphalted highway, he roared along at the head of a grand procession from one end of the road to the other. A bottle of champagne and a ribbon across the highway awaited Penrose's arrival at the Broadmoor end, but he ran his big white Pierce Arrow off the road just before he reached them.

In the mid-1930's, not long before he died, Penrose built a large tower above his zoo on top of Cheyenne Mountain. The tower was to be called "Penrose Memorial," but his friends asked him why tourists from Oklahoma would pay toll-road fees to see the grave of a man they never had heard of. So Penrose demurred and named the tower instead the "Will Rogers Shrine of the Sun," after his idol, who had just been killed. The fact that the monument was named for another didn't bother Penrose in the least, and he left orders that his ashes were to be placed in a crypt on top of the mountain that looked down on a monument more fitting to the flamboyant millionaire—the five-thousand-acre, multimillion-dollar, pink-tinted complex, the Broadmoor.

The Count's Casino, built in 1891, burned in 1897 (*Denver Public Library Western Collection*).

191

The first casino was replaced with a less pretentious one, now the Broadmoor Golf Club (*Denver Public Library Western Collection*). Railroad tracks were built right up to the hotel to facilitate construction (*Bob McIntyre, Broadmoor Hotel*).

The lobby with curved marble staircase, about the time the Broadmoor opened. The Georgian ballroom had marble pilasters, plum-colored hangings, and crystal chandeliers (*Denver Public Library Western Collection*).

The palm court (*Denver Public Library Western Collection*). The original Broadmoor (*below*), at right; the Broadmoor South, built recently, left.

The Broadmoor complex today. One of the latest Broadmoor acquisitions is the Golden Bee, an English pub which was dismantled and shipped to this country. The bar and most of the decorations are authentic, the rest are period reproductions—the etched-glass doors, designed from old photographs, and the pressed-metal ceiling.

BIBLIOGRAPHY

I BOOKS AND PAMPHLETS

Anonymous. *City of Pueblo and the State of Colorado, The*. Pueblo, Geo. W. Engelhardt & Co., 1890.

———. *Colorado: American Guide Series*. New York, Hastings House, 1941.

———. *Cripple Creek and Colorado Springs Illustrated*. Colorado Springs, Warren & Stride, 1896.

———. *Leadville: The City of the Skies*. Salida, The Western Guide Publishing Co., 1928.

———. *Review of Colorado's Enterprising Cities*. Denver, Jno. Lethem, 1893.

———. *Sketch of the Pueblos*. Pueblo, Board of Trade, 1883.

———. *Souvenir: Central City, Black Hawk, Nevadaville*. Denver, The Western Newspaper Union, *c*. 1899.

Arps, Louisa A. *Chalk Creek, Colorado*. Denver, John Van Male, 1940.

———. *Denver in Slices*. Denver, Sage Books, 1959.

Bailey, Vernon Howe. *The Broadmoor*. Denver, W. H. Kistler Co., 1918.

Bancroft, Caroline. *Brown Palace in Denver, The*. Boulder, Johnson Publishing Co., 1960.

———. *Famous Aspen*. Boulder, Johnson Publishing Co., 1951.

———. *Glenwood's Early Glamor*. Boulder, Johnson Publishing Co., 1958.

———. *Guide to Central City*. Denver, The World Press, Inc., 1946.

———. *Gulch of Gold*. Denver, Sage Books, 1958.

Beebe, Lucius, and Charles Clegg. *The American West*. New York, E. P. Dutton & Co., 1955.

Beshoar, Barron B. *Out of the Depths*. Denver, Golden Bell Press, n.d.

Bowles, Samuel. *In Parks and Mountains of Colorado*. n.p., 1886.

Boyd, David. *Greeley and the Union Colony*. Greeley, The Greeley Tribune Press, 1890.

Buchanan, John W. and Doris G. *A Story of the Fabulous Windsor Hotel*. Denver, The A. B. Hirschfeld Press, 1944.

Carothers, June E. *Estes Park: Past and Present*. Denver, The University of Denver Press, 1951.

Cather, Willa. *A Lost Lady*. New York, Alfred A. Knopf, 1923.

Crofutt, George A. *Crofutt's Grip-Sack Guide of Colorado*. Omaha, The Overland Publishing Co., 1881.

Crum, Josie Moore. *Ouray County, Colorado*. Durango, San Juan History, Inc., 1962.

Daniels, Bettie Marie, and Virginia McConnel. *The Springs of Manitou*. Denver, Sage Books, 1964.

Dunning, Marion Harold. *Over Hill and Vale*. 2 vols. Boulder, Johnson Publishing Co., 1962.

Eberhart, Perry. *Guide to the Colorado Ghost Towns and Mining Camps*. Denver, Sage Books, 1959.

Everett, George G., and Dr. Wendell F. Hutchinson. *Under the Angel of Shavano*. Denver, Golden Bell Press, 1963.

Fossett, Frank. *Colorado: Tourist's Guide to the Rocky Mountains*. New York, C. G. Crawford, 1879.

Griswold, Don and Jean. *A Carbonate Camp Called Leadville*. Denver, University of Denver Press, 1951.

Halliday, Brett. *Denver Murders*. New York, Duell, Sloan and Pearce, 1946.

Harrison, Louise C. *Empire and the Berthoud Pass*. Denver, Big Mountain Press, 1964.

Hollenback, Frank R. *Central City and Black Hawk, Colorado: Then and Now*. Denver, Sage Books, 1961.

Hunt, Inez, and Wanetta W. Draper. *To Colorado's Restless Ghosts*. Denver, Sage Books, 1960.

Jarvis, Marion. *The Strater Hotel Story*. Durango, n.d.

Lamborn, Alfred. *Stanley Hotels at Estes Park, Colorado, U.S.A.* n.p., 1922.

Lee, Mabel Barbee. *Cripple Creek Days*. Garden City, Doubleday & Co., Inc., 1958.

Maass, John. *The Gingerbread Age*. New York, Bramhall House, 1957.

McFarland, Mrs. Louis Dupuy. (Unpublished MS in the Colorado State Historical Society.)

Manning, J. F. *Visions of Victor*. The Merchants Publishing Co., n.d.

Montgomery, Mabel Guise. *A Story of Gold Hill Colorado*, n.p., 1930.

Olsen, Mary Ann. *The Silverton Story*. Cortez, Beaber Printing Co., 1962.

Pourtales, James. *Lessons Learned from Experience*. Colorado Springs, Colorado College, 1955.

Smith, Don. *Chalk Creek to the Past*. n.p., 1958.

Sprague, Marshall. *Money Mountain*. Boston, Little, Brown and Co., 1953.

———. *Newport in the Rockies*. Denver, Sage Books, 1961.

State Historical Society of Colorado and The National Society of the Colonial Dames of America in the State of Colorado. *Hotel De Paris and Louis Dupuy in Georgetown, Colorado*. Boulder, Johnson Publishing Co., 1954.

Wallace, Betty. *Gunnison: A Short Illustrated History*. Denver, Sage Books, 1964.

Wentworth, Frank. *Aspen on the Roaring Fork*. Lakewood, Francis B. Rizzari, 1950.

Willison, George F. *Here They Dug the Gold*. New York, Reynal & Hitchcock, 1946.

Wolle, Muriel Sibell. *Stampede to Timberline*. Denver, Sage Books, 1949.

Wood, Myron and Nancy. *West to Durango*. Colorado Springs, Chaparral Press, 1964.

Wright, Carolyn and Clarence. *Tiny Hinsdale of the Silvery San Juans*. Denver, Big Mountain Press, 1964.

NEWSPAPERS AND PERIODICALS

Aspen Daily Chronicle
Aspen Times Weekly
Boulder Daily Camera
Boulder Miner and Farmer
Canon City Daily Record
Colorado Magazine
Craig Empire Courier
Creede Candle
Cripple Creek Times
Denver Post
Denver Republican
Denver Times
Denver Tribune
Empire Daily News
Evening Star (Cripple Creek)
Gazette Telegraph (Colorado Springs)
Georgetown Courier
Grand Junction Sentinel
Great Divide
Greeley Sunday Journal
Gunnison News-Champion
Leadville Herald-Democrat
Pueblo Chieftain
Pueblo Star-Journal
Register-Call (Central City)
Rocky Mountain News
Steamboat Pilot

INDEX

(Places are in Colorado unless otherwise noted)

University of Oklahoma Press
Norman